S E R I E S

A NavPress Bible study on the book of

EPHESIANS

NAVPRESS
A MINISTRY OF THE NAVIGATORS
P.O. BOX 35001, COLORADO SPRINGS, COLORADO 80935

The Navigators is an international Christian organization. Jesus Christ gave His followers the Great Commission to go and make disciples (Matthew 28:19). The aim of The Navigators is to help fulfill that commission by multiplying laborers for Christ in every nation.

NavPress is the publishing ministry of The Navigators. NavPress publications are tools to help Christians grow. Although publications alone cannot make disciples or change lives, they can help believers learn biblical discipleship, and apply what they learn to their lives and ministries.

Most Scripture quotations are from the *Holy Bible: New International Version* (NIV). Copyright © 1973, 1978, 1984, International Bible Society. Used by permission of Zondervan Bible Publishers. Other versions used are the *New American Standard Bible* (NASB), © The Lockman Foundation 1960, 1962, 1963, 1968, 1971, 1972, 1973, 1975, 1977; the *Revised Standard Version of the Bible* (RSV), copyrighted 1946, 1952 © 1971, 1973; and the *King James Version* (KJV).

Printed in the United States of America

15 16 17 18 19 20 21 22 23/99 98 97 96 95

FOR A FREE CATALOG OF
NAVPRESS BOOKS & BIBLE STUDIES,
CALL 1-800-366-7788 (USA)
or 1-416-499-4615 (CANADA)

CONTENTS

ACKNOWLEDGMENTS

This LIFECHANGE study has been produced through the coordinated efforts of a team of Navigator Bible study developers and NavPress editorial staff, along with a nationwide network of fieldtesters.

SERIES EDITOR: KAREN HINCKLEY

HOW TO USE THIS STUDY

Objectives

Each guide in the LIFECHANGE series of Bible studies covers one book of the Bible. Although the LIFECHANGE guides vary with the individual books they explore, they share some common goals:

1. To provide you with a firm foundation of understanding and a thirst to return to the book;
2. To teach you by example how to study a book of the Bible without structured guides;
3. To give you all the historical background, word definitions, and explanatory notes you need, so that your only other reference is the Bible;
4. To help you grasp the message of the book as a whole;
5. To teach you how to let God's Word transform you into Christ's image.

Each lesson in this study is designed to take 60 to 90 minutes to complete on your own. The guide is based on the assumption that you are completing one lesson per week, but if time is limited you can do half a lesson per week or whatever amount allows you to be thorough.

Flexibility

LIFECHANGE guides are flexible, allowing you to adjust the quantity and depth of your study to meet your individual needs. The guide offers many optional questions in addition to the regular numbered questions. The optional questions, which appear in the margins of the study pages, include the following:

Optional Application. Nearly all application questions are optional; we hope you will do as many as you can without overcommitting yourself.

For Thought and Discussion. Beginning Bible students should be able to handle these, but even advanced students need to think about them. These questions frequently deal with ethical issues and other biblical principles. They often offer cross-references to spark thought, but the references do not give obvious answers. They are good for group discussions.

For Further Study. These include: a) cross-references that shed light on a topic the book discusses, and b) questions that delve deeper into the passage. You can omit them to shorten a lesson without missing a major point of the passage.

(Note: At the end of lessons three through thirteen you are given the option of outlining the passage just studied. Although the outline is optional, you will almost surely find it worthwhile.)

If you are meeting in a group, decide together which optional questions to prepare for each lesson, and how much of the lesson you will cover at the next meeting. Normally, the group leader should make this decision, but you might let each member choose his own application questions.

As you grow in your walk with God, you will find the LIFECHANGE guide growing with you—a helpful reference on a topic, a continuing challenge for application, a source of questions for many levels of growth.

Overview and Details

The guide begins with an overview of the book. The key to interpretation is context—what is the whole passage or book *about*?—and the key to context is purpose—what is the author's *aim* for the whole work? In lesson one you will lay the foundation for your study by asking yourself, Why did the author (and God) write the book? What did they want to accomplish? What is the book about?

Then, in lesson two, you will begin analyzing successive passages in detail. Thinking about how a paragraph fits into the overall goal of the book will help you to see its purpose. Its purpose will help you see its meaning. Frequently reviewing a chart or outline of the book will enable you to make these connections.

Finally, in the last lesson, you will review the whole book, returning to the big picture to see whether your view of it has changed after closer study. Review will also strengthen your grasp of major issues and give you an idea of how you have grown from your study.

Kinds of Questions

Bible study on your own—without a structured guide—follows a progression. First you observe: What does the passage *say*? Then you interpret: What does the passage *mean*? Lastly you apply: How does this truth affect my life? The act of wording a question for the guide nearly always makes it interpretation, however, so you may want to observe first yourself.

Some of the "how" and "why" questions will take some creative thinking, even prayer, to answer. Some are opinion questions without clearcut right answers; these will lend themselves to discussions and side studies.

Don't let your study become an exercise of knowledge alone. Treat the passage as God's Word, and stay in dialogue with Him as you study. Pray, "Lord, what do you want me to see here?" "Father, why is this true?" "Lord, how does this apply to my life?"

It is important that you write down your answers. The act of writing clarifies your thinking and helps you to remember.

Meditating on verses is an option in several lessons. Its purpose is to let biblical truth sink into your inner convictions so that you will increasingly be able to act on this truth as a natural way of life. You may want to find a quiet place to spend five minutes each day repeating the verse(s) to yourself. Think about what each word, phrase, and sentence means to you. During the rest of the day, remind yourself of the verse(s) at intervals.

Study Aids

A list of reference materials, including a few notes of explanation to help you make good use of them, begins on page 123. This guide is designed to include enough background to let you interpret with just your Bible and the guide. Still, if you want more information on a subject or want to study a book on your own, try the references listed.

Scripture Versions

Unless otherwise indicated, the Bible quotations in this guide are from the New International Version of the Bible. Other versions cited are the Revised Standard Version (RSV) and the New American Standard Bible (NASB).

Use any translation you like for study, preferably more than one. A paraphrase, such as the Living Bible or the Good News Bible, is not accurate enough for study, but it can be helpful for comparison or devotional reading.

Memorizing and Meditating

A Psalmist wrote, "I have hidden your word in my heart that I might not sin against you" (Psalm 119:11). If you write down a verse or passage that challenges or encourages you, and reflect on it often for a week or more, you will find it beginning to affect your motives and actions. We forget quickly what we read once; we remember what we ponder.

When you find a significant verse or passage, you might copy it onto a card to keep with you. Set aside five minutes during each day just to think about what the passage might mean in your life. Recite it over to yourself, exploring its meaning. Then, return to your passage as often as you can during your day, for a brief review. You will soon find it coming to mind spontaneously.

For Group Study

A group of four to ten people allows the richest discussions, but you can adapt this guide for other sized groups. It will suit a wide range of group types, such as home Bible studies, growth groups, youth groups, and businessmen's studies. Both new and experienced Bible students, new and mature Christians, will benefit from the guide. You can omit or leave for later years any questions you find too easy or too hard.

The guide is intended to lead a group through one lesson per week. However, feel free to split lessons if you want to discuss them more thoroughly. Or, omit some questions in a lesson if preparation or discussion time is limited. You can always return to this guide for personal study later on. You will be able to discuss only a few questions at length, so choose some for discussion and others for background. Make time at each discussion for members to ask about anything that gave them trouble.

Each lesson in the guide ends with a section called *For the Group*. These sections give advice on how to focus a discussion, how you might apply the lesson in your group, how you might shorten a lesson, and so on. The group leader should read each *For the Group* at least a week ahead so that he or she can tell the group how to prepare for the next lesson.

Each member should prepare for a meeting by writing answers for all the background and discussion questions to be covered. If the group decides not to take an hour per week for private preparation, then expect to take at least two meetings per lesson to work through the questions. Application will be very difficult, however, without private thought and prayer.

Two reasons for studying in a group are accountability and support. When each member commits in front of the rest to seek growth in an area of life, you can pray with one another, listen jointly for God's guidance, help one another to resist temptation, assure each other that the other's growth matters to you, use the group to practice spiritual principles, and so on. Pray about one another's commitments and needs at most meetings. Spend the first few minutes of each meeting sharing any results from applications prompted by previous lessons. Then discuss new applications toward the end of the meeting. Follow such sharing with prayer for these and other needs.

If you write down each other's applications and prayer requests, you are more likely to remember to pray for them during the week, ask about them next meeting, and notice answered prayers. You might want to get a notebook for prayer requests and discussion notes.

Notes taken during discussion will help you to remember, follow up on ideas, stay on the subject, and clarify a total view of an issue. But don't let note-taking keep you from participating. Some groups choose one member at each meeting to take notes. Then someone copies the notes and distributes them at the next meeting. Rotating these tasks can help include people. Some groups have someone take notes on a large pad of paper or erasable marker board (preformed shower wallboard works well), so that everyone can see what has been recorded.

Page 126 lists some good sources of counsel for leading group studies. The *Small Group Letter*, published by NavPress, is unique, offering insights from experienced leaders every other month.

PAUL AND EPHESUS

Map of the Roman Empire

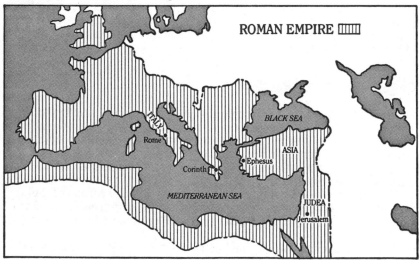

The part of the world now known as Turkey basked in prosperity during the first century AD. As one of the older, more stable provinces of the Roman Empire, it seemed far from the turmoil of border provinces like Palestine and Gaul. Agriculture, industry and commerce all flourished under Roman protection, and travel was safe, although still expensive.

Asia boasted seven urban centers, of which the queen was Ephesus. Through her port passed goods from China and inland Asia Minor bound for Italy. Wide avenues, huge public buildings and squares, and luxurious private homes were designed to impress tourists. The theater could hold 25,000 people. Dozens of temples used color and symbols to attract the eye, and the greatest of these, dedicated to Artemis of the Ephesians, was known throughout the Empire as one of the Seven Wonders of the World. It was four times the size of the Parthenon.

Powerful and powerless

A hundred local aristocrats controlled the city council of Ephesus, which governed the city for Rome. These men also owned most of the surrounding land and the major industries, and so were fabulously rich.

However, the strength of the city was its large class of merchants, businessmen, and craftsmen. Some were rich, but never so rich as the aristocrats. This "middle class" was highly mobile; a slave-craftsman might well become a prosperous free businessman. Trade associations organized wealthy owners with poor craftsmen, free citizens with resident aliens and slaves. However, everyone was acutely aware of his own and others' social status at any moment.

In political power, every non-aristocrat was equal—equally powerless. Yet, as long as trade and industry prospered, people accepted the system. Occasionally a riot or strike flared when a particular group felt threatened economically, but these were quickly controlled. The urban poor were quieted by a combination of strict discipline with free bread and entertainment. Tenant farmers on aristocrats' estates were isolated.

Religion for propaganda

Asian cities comprised dozens of ethnic groups with often contradictory social and economic systems. The Jewish population of Asia was the fourth largest in the Empire. Rome encouraged ethnic groups to mix, believing that people would be more docile if they thought of themselves as members of one world order. Hence, propaganda about the Roman Peace abounded, and religious and philosophical ideas supported it.

The Roman cult of the emperor was an attempt to foster patriotism, but it affected civic leaders almost exclusively. It touched ordinary people only when they had to offer incense to the emperor's personal guardian deity during an oath.

Roman state religion was distinct from the emperor cult. However, it was just as indifferent to heartfelt faith; it was a system of precise rites done to gain the favor of supernatural powers for the community. "Piety" meant the faithful fulfillment of duties. Personal or mystical religious experience, magic, and anything new won disapproval.

Syncretism

On the other hand, Romans were always open to rites long used to please previously unknown powers. They especially admired anything which seemed Greek, but they absorbed the practices of most of the peoples they conquered.

Originally, each ethnic group had had its own local cult, none of which claimed authority outside a specific place. However, when Greeks had moved east or Asians west, they had brought their gods. In the cities, peoples had lived side by side, each with their own religions. Over time, though, the ties to place of origin weakened. Neighbors had to come to terms with each other's practices, and since no one claimed exclusive truth, people easily translated foreign ways into their own idioms. They understood gods with vaguely similar traits to be the same gods with various names. Thus, the Greeks called the Asian fertility goddess "Artemis," and assigned to her the traits of both Greek and Asian tradition. The Romans understood her as "Diana" by the same process. Cult practices were also borrowed, as people learned what seemed equally valid ways of worshipping a god. This mixing of Greek and eastern religions is called *syncretism*.

Style without substance

Ephesus had temples dedicated to gods with Greek, Roman, Egyptian, Asian, and Persian names, or combinations thereof like "Zeus-Sarapis." Each temple had its priests with colored robes and shaven heads available to explain the myth of the god and to accept sacrifices. Butcher shops were connected with temples to sell the meat after the ritual slaughter. However, incense was replacing animal sacrifice except for festivals. Daily worship with hymns, prayers, lamps, and incense had become common for the most popular cults, and sermons might be preached on special days. Yet, with rare exceptions, the old gods were losing the deep attachment of the people. The state still supported them, and rich men showed their wealth by financing magnificent temples, but most people had enthusiasm only for the elaborate festivals, processions, and games with which cults vied for attention.

Paul's conversion

Paul was a Jew by birth, but a Jew of a curious sort. He was born in the first decade AD in Tarsus, a small but prosperous city on the trade route from Syria to Asia Minor. Somehow, Paul obtained educations both in the Greek disciplines of rhetoric and classical literature and in the Pharisaic approach to Jewish law. He must have attended Greek schools with Gentiles (non-Jews) and learned about God in a synagogue of Greek-speaking Pharisees. His "Bible" would have been the *Septuagint*, the Jewish Scriptures in Greek.

The word *Pharisee* comes from a Hebrew word which means "the separated ones," for the Pharisees felt God had set them apart to study and live by *Torah* (the Law, or Teaching, of Moses). They expected a *Messiah* (Hebrew for "Anointed One," Greek: *Christ*, the Savior God would send to liberate Israel), but one very different from Jesus. Thus when some Jews began to preach that Jesus was the Messiah, many Pharisees fought them furiously.

But around 35 AD, Jesus confronted Paul in a blinding encounter (Acts 9:1-19), revealing to Paul that he was persecuting the very God he professed to worship. Paul's life now turned from a Pharisaic observance of God's

11

law to a devoted obedience to Jesus Christ, the revealed Messiah. Paul realized that because of Jesus, Pharisaic law-keeping was no longer necessary and could even conflict with God's will. He joined the very faction of Jews he had been persecuting. Soon after, God commissioned him to proclaim the Messiah not just to those who were already God's chosen, but also to those who had not known Him.

Paul in Ephesus

Paul had been a missionary for about seventeen years before he reached Ephesus (Acts 18:19-21). After two of his fellow-missionaries had prepared the ground for several months, Paul came and set up his customary headquarters for long-term evangelism in a province (Acts 19-20). With the colleagues he brought with him and with some Christians already in Ephesus, he founded a network of house-churches. This network eventually spread to several cities in Asia.

Paul's first converts were probably Jews and "God-fearers." "God-fearer" was the Jewish term for Gentiles who wanted to follow the worship and ethics of the Lord but did not want to formally renounce their culture nor undergo circumcision. Most new Christians would have been members of the middle class looking for truth and security, but probably not for a total change in lifestyle and attitudes. Individuals might have independently committed their lives to Jesus, but slaves and women were not very free to choose a religion. On the other hand, if a head of a household decided to follow Christ, his children, wife, slaves, and clients often did so with him. Thus, the infant church in a town was built of households, all meeting in the home of one of its more prosperous members. As a church outgrew a house, some households broke off to meet in another home.

Paul and his team spent two and a half years in Ephesus making converts and training leaders to take responsibility once the mission team left. While in Ephesus, Paul wrote letters to some of the similar church-networks he had founded earlier (in Galatia, Corinth, etc.), practical letters in which he tried to settle disputes of church policy.

Paul's letter to Ephesus

After leaving Ephesus, Paul applied himself to unifying the churches he had already established into one Church, but a trip to Jerusalem led to his imprisonment first there and eventually in Rome (Acts 21:27—28:31). After some two years he was probably released, about 60 AD. Two or three years later, he was rearrested and returned to Rome, where he probably wrote this letter to Ephesus. The Roman authorities tried and executed him shortly thereafter.

Since many of the best early manuscripts do not include the words "in Ephesus" in the first sentence of the letter, many scholars believe that Paul wrote it to circulate among the churches in several Asian cities. Other scholars think that the letter was for those gentile Christians in Ephesus, and perhaps in other cities, who had become believers after Paul left. Either of these theories would explain why Paul addressed his readers as though he had never met them.

OVERVIEW AND EPHESIANS 1:1-2

To the Saints

Before you get immersed in the details of Paul's words, take an overview of the whole letter. Potentially confusing verses will be clearer later if you can see how they fit into Paul's overall message.

First impressions

1. The best preparation for grasping Ephesians is to read it through several times, comparing various versions. Try reading it aloud. Get a general impression.

2. Describe the mood (tone, feeling) of the letter. (Is Paul formal, intimate, angry, jubilant . . . ? Is he writing a story, a personal message, a sermon . . . ? Is he describing, giving direction, trying to persuade?) If the mood changes anywhere, note where it changes.

_____

_____

_____

_____

_____

_____

_____

3. Repetition is a clue to the ideas a writer considers most important to his message. What words or ideas occur over and over in Paul's letter?

_____

_____

_____

Broad outline

4. Reread the letter, preferably in a fresh translation. This time, think of a short phrase or sentence to describe what each main section of the book is about. (These major sections are probably groups of paragraphs.)

1:1-2 *Paul greets the saints.*

1:3-14 _____

_____

1:15-23 _____

_____

2:1-10 _____

_____

2:11-22 _____

_____

3:1-13 _____

_____

3:14-21 _____

_____

4:1-16 _____

_____

4:17-32 _____

_____

5:1-20 _____

_____

5:21-6:9 _____

_____

6:10-20 _____

_____

6:21-24 _____

5. Paul's message seems to divide into two main sections, chapters 1-3 and 4-6. What do you think each section is about? What does the purpose of each seem to be?

1-3 _____

_____

_____

4-6 _____

_____

_____

Theme/purpose

6. What do you think was Paul's reason for writing this letter? What does its content suggest he was trying to accomplish?

_____

_____

_____

_____

_____

_____

7. Try to state the main message of Paul's letter in one sentence. Think about the themes of each half

15

of the letter. If you need more than one sentence at this point, use more.

_____

_____

_____

_____

_____

_____

8. If you have not already done so, read the historical background on pages 9-12. Is there any information that seems particularly helpful to you in understanding the book of Ephesians? Please explain briefly.

_____

_____

_____

_____

_____

_____

Study Skill—Bible Study Aids
If you would like to study the background of Ephesians in greater depth, consult one of the sources listed on pages 123-127. These and similar commentaries will also be quite helpful to you if you decide to study another book of the Bible on your own.

Greetings

Jewish letters of Paul's day commonly opened with a sentence giving the titles of sender and addressee. Then came a sentence wishing peace and blessings to the addressee.

An *apostle* (verse 1) is "one who is sent." In its

narrow sense, the word meant one of a small group of men whom the church recognized as having special authority from God to clarify the policy and teaching of the whole body. Paul may have been the only one of this group who was not one of Jesus' disciples, and he was conscious of his status.

Saints (verse 1) were literally, "holy ones." The Greek Old Testament used the word for the people of Israel—God's chosen. Paul included all whom God had made holy, even gentile believers in Christ.

Grace (verse 2) is "favor shown by a superior to an inferior."[1] It is especially God's free decision to include the Gentiles into His people. But Paul mentioned other gracious gifts in his letter (3:7, 4:7, 4:11). He used this term of God's kindness to humanity instead of the usual Greek greeting *rejoice* and in addition to the Jewish *peace*.

Peace (verse 2) is "wholeness," that is, "a gift of God affecting the totality of psychic, physical, personal, familial, economic, and political dimensions of man's life."[2] Like grace, peace referred to social relationships, man-man and man-God. According to the Old Testament prophets, peace would be fulfilled when the Messiah ruled.

For Thought and Discussion: What do you think Paul wanted to communicate by describing himself and his readers as in verse 1?

9. Is there any part of this lesson that specifically touches upon an area of your life in which you'd like to make a change? If so, write it down here, and try to come up with some practical way you could begin to work on this area with God's help.

_____

_____

_____

_____

_____

_____

_____

10. In your initial readings of Paul's letter to the Ephesians, you may have come across concepts you'd like clarified or questions you'd like answered as you go deeper into this study. While

17

Optional Application: Consider Paul's concern for Christians he did not know personally, and his sense of responsibility toward them as an apostle of Christ. Do you have any responsibility for the spiritual integrity of other believers? If so, in what areas do you feel qualified to help them?

In what areas do you feel yourself lacking, but would like to grow so you could help others?

your thoughts are still fresh, you may want to jot down your questions here to serve as personal objectives for your investigation of this letter.

_____

_____

_____

_____

_____

_____

_____

For the group

Unless you already know each other well, you might spend some time in your next few meetings establishing trust, common ground, and a sense of where each person is coming from. This may help you to discuss frankly how Ephesians applies to you later on. This meeting, share something of your histories—for example, what you remember about being nine years old, or the first place you lived. Discussing question 9 or the "Optional Application" will help to show each other how you see yourselves.

Compare your passage titles and theme statement to those in the chart on page 19. There is no one right answer, so discuss why you prefer one title to another. Group members who felt successful with these projects should share how they went about thinking of titles and seeing themes.

1. Markus Barth, *Ephesians 1-3*, Anchor Bible Volume 34 (Garden City, New York: Doubleday and Company, Inc., 1974), page 74.
2. Barth, page 74.

Chart of Ephesians

Paul's theme: Know who you are before God through Christ, and live according to that identity.

		1:1-2 Paul greets the saints.
The Foundation	**Know who you are before God through Christ**	1:3-14 Paul praises God for His preplanned spiritual blessings.
		1:15-23 Paul prays that we would understand these blessings.
		2:1-10 Paul teaches the individual's new position because of God's blessings.
		2:11-22 Paul teaches the group's new position because of God's blessings.
		3:1-13 Paul explains his own mission: to proclaim God's blessings.
		3:14-21 Paul prays that we would know God's blessings in our deepest being.
The Application	**Live Christ-centered lives because of your new identity**	4:1-16 Paul urges unity based on the common foundation.
		4:17-32 Paul urges holiness based on the common foundation.
		5:1-20 Paul urges a walk in love, light, and wisdom based on the common foundation.
		5:21-6:9 Paul urges submission based on the common foundation.
		6:10-20 Paul urges steadfast warfare against spiritual forces based on the common foundation.
		6:21-24 Paul closes.

EPHESIANS 1:3-14

Praise

A house-church's weekly meetings were patterned on those of a Hellenistic synagogue. The people might have shared a meal and probably celebrated the *Eucharist*, the commemoration of the Last Supper. Most of the meetings were spent singing hymns, hearing passages of Jewish Scripture read, discussing and hearing teaching about the Scripture, and praying.

Oral readings were not spoken, but rather intoned as chant. Because of the musical quality of Greek vowels, the language was more easily understood in public addresses when intoned. Thus, readings had hymn-like effects. Prayer, too, was intoned, with a cantor singing a line and the people responding.

The service was not performed for the congregation; instead, all those present—whether male or female, slave or merchant—participated. A member or a visiting prophet might have delivered a prophecy of encouragement or rebuke. A traveling teacher might have spoken; or a letter, such as Paul's, might have been intoned.

1. Read 1:3-14, preferably at least once silently and once aloud. If you did not know that the passage was part of a letter, but had just heard it read or sung in church, what would you think it was? What effect in the hearts of his hearers do you think Paul wanted to produce?

_____

_____

For Further Study:
Using cross-references and Bible study aids, do your own word study on Paul's key phrase. Summarize your results by writing here what *you* think Paul means by this term.

_____

_____

_____

2. What key phrase does Paul repeat in various ways in this passage?

_____

_____

_____

3. What does verse 3 say the Father has done for us?

_____

_____

_____

_____

_____

4. List the blessings Paul named in the rest of the passage. (If you like, personalize them by writing "me" instead of "us.")

verse 4 _____

_____

_____

_____

verse 5 _____

_____

_____

_____

22

verse 7 _____

_____

_____

verse 9 _____

_____

_____

verses 11-12 _____

_____

_____

verses 13-14 _____

_____

_____

_____

For Further Study:
Study 1:3-14 for yourself. Do you agree with the analysis of the passage's structure in the Study Skill below? Why or why not?

Study Skill—Structure
A passage's overall structure helps to reveal what the author is driving at. In 1:3-14, Paul's theme seems to be what God has done for us "in" or "through" Christ. Paul evidently began with a summary of the Father's work for us (verse 3) and then listed specifics. (We arrive at this conclusion by reading the passage over and over, looking for the broad flow of the argument, and asking, "how is this organized?")

Holy: (verse 4). Set apart utterly for God, with the character and conduct befitting such a state. The inner nature, transformed by grace, is central to holiness, for only the holy can approach the Holy One. Holiness, like adoption, is a relationship to God.

For Further Study:
For more on adoption (verse 5), look up the word in a concordance (see page 124). Some references you will find are Romans 8:14-17 and Galatians 3:26, 4:1-7.

For Further Study:
How does Jesus' blood redeem us? (See Hebrews 9:1-10:18; Exodus 12:1-4,13; Leviticus 16:1-34; Deuteronomy 21:1-9; Romans 3:21-26. A good book on this subject is Robert E. Coleman's *The New Covenant* [NavPress, 1984].)

5. *Paraphrasing*—putting Scripture into your own words—helps to assure that you understand it. Put verse 4 into your own words.

_____

_____

_____

_____

_____

Redemption: (verse 7). A releasing from slavery or death penalty on payment of a ransom. In this case, freedom from the penalty of sin (rebellion against God).

6. According to verses 7-8, how are we enabled to become holy and blameless? Use your own words. (*Optional:* Use 2 Corinthians 3:17-18 as a cross-reference.)

_____

_____

_____

_____

_____

_____

7. Paul repeated three times God's purpose in bestowing these blessings (verses 5-6,12,14). What result does Paul teach that God expects in our lives?

_____

_____

_____

_____

_____

_____

For Further Study:
Paul said in verses 5 and 11 that God "predestined" Christians to become His heirs. In verse 13 he said his readers became Christians when they heard and believed the gospel. Belief implies a decision freely chosen. Explain as best you can how both of Paul's statements are true. (This issue has taxed the minds of Christians for centuries. Don't worry that you cannot fully explain the contrasts.)[2]

When the times will have reached their fulfillment
(verse 10). "The dawning of a new period in which God's promise and law . . . are fulfilled."[1] That is, when Christ returns. (Note: Unless otherwise marked, all biblical quotations are from the New International Version.)

---

8. According to verse 10, what is God's ultimate goal? Explain in your own words. (*Optional:* See also Philippians 2:9-11 and Colossians 1:19-20.)

_____

_____

_____

_____

_____

_____

9. In verse 13, Paul says that God has guaranteed His blessings are secure by "sealing" us with the Holy Spirit. What do you think it means to be "sealed" in Christ with the Spirit? (*Optional:* John 14:16, Romans 8:15-17, 2 Corinthians 1:22, Esther 8:8.)

_____

_____

_____

_____

_____

_____

_____

Optional Application: Choose one of the blessings for which Paul praised God. Name at least three implications this blessing has for your life (attitudes about yourself or other people, action you should take, priorities). (For instance, "If I really believe that God so unshakably loves me that he has adopted me permanently, knowing beforehand all I will be and do, then . . . .") This week, memorize and meditate on the verse(s) involved, and look for ways that it can begin to take hold in your life.

Your response

The last step of Bible study is asking yourself, "What difference does the passage make to my life? How should it make me think or act?" Applications require time, thought, prayer, and sometimes even discussion with another person. Thorough and specific decision on one application will produce more growth than listing many applications without reflection or commitment.

    Question 10 gives you a chance to choose your own application of 1:3-14. The "Optional Application" on this page offers a suggested application, if you prefer to use it rather than coming up with one on your own.

10. Is there a specific response you would like to make to 1:3-14?

    _____

    _____

    _____

    _____

_____

_____

_____

Following Paul's example

11. Why do you think Paul put praise first in his
letter?

_____

_____

_____

_____

_____

12. a. Do you ever find it difficult to praise God in
prayer, especially for more than a minute at a
time? If so, why?

_____

_____

_____

_____

_____

_____

_____

b. How could you overcome these obstacles?

_____

_____

_____

_____

_____

_____

_____

_____

Take time now to praise God with the particular aspects of His character and actions that inspire you from your study of Ephesians 1:3-14.

For the group

After everyone is clear on what 1:3-14 is about and what each blessing means, discuss what the blessings mean to each of you (question 10). If you tackle the optional question on page 25, don't expect to fully resolve it.

Take time at the end of your meeting to praise God, especially if you discuss questions 11 and 12.

The "One God" of Paganism

The notion of one Power governing the whole cosmos fit well with the Empire's vision of one world social, political, and economic order. A single deity behind all the cults explained the common features. Concepts of that deity varied, however. Some people conceived of one hierarchy of divine beings, perhaps with a supreme god at the top. Others thought of one god with many names. Stoic philosophy described the impersonal force of the *Logos*, Highest Reason, by which the cosmos functioned. Stoics taught that man must know and conform to the ethical principles of that Reason in order to live well, for *Logos*, not human choice, determined all events. Finally, some people believed in *Tyche*, the personified Fate who was not blind but irrational and malevolent.

---

1. Barth, page 88.
2. The Bible's thorough discussion of predestination and free will is Paul's letter to the Romans, especially chapters 2-11. You'll find helpful treatments of this subject in Martin Luther's *The Bondage of the Will*, John Calvin's *Institutes* (the chapter on predestination), and Stephen Charnock's *The Being and Attributes of God* (chapters on God's wisdom and knowledge).

EPHESIANS 1:15-23

Thanksgiving and Prayer

Again, read through the whole passage at least once before beginning the questions. Then review the theme of the letter and your title for 1:15-23 to orient yourself. You might also want to skim the questions before answering any.

1. *Connecting words* are clues to how passages relate to each other. What does "For this reason" in verse 15 tell you?

   _____

   _____

   _____

   _____

   _____

Faith: (verse 15). Not the mental state of belief in certain doctrines, but the moral attitude of faithfulness; that is, the attitude which follows from personal surrender to God.

2. For what did Paul give thanks (verses 15-16)?

   _____

   _____

For Thought and Discussion: Why is it important that the truths of question 3 become "heart" knowledge, not just "head" knowledge?

_____

_____

Wisdom and revelation: (verse 17). The ability "not only to learn but also to teach . . . the revealed secret to others."[1]

For Thought and Discussion: Think about what it means to have "the eyes of your heart enlightened." How might this help you to more fully know your hope, inheritance, and power (verses 18-19)?

Know: (verse 17). "Real, deep, and full knowledge, as distinct from awareness or superficial acquaintance."[2] Biblical knowledge is intimate relationship, as opposed to grasp of facts.

3. What did Paul pray that the Ephesians would come to know increasingly deeply?

   verse 17 _____

   _____

   verse 18 _____

   _____

   verse 18 _____

   _____

   _____

   verse 19 _____

   _____

Heart: (verse 18). The seat of a person's thought, will, and emotions; the center of his being; his deep mind.

Hope: (verse 18). Not the mood of the one who hopes, but the content of a sure expectation.

4. This section of the first chapter of Ephesians treats several weighty themes. In order to gain a fuller understanding of Paul's rich teaching in this passage, study the following cross-references and note what you learn about each topic.

Your hope in Christ (verse 18)

Note especially the *content* of and the *response* to hope.

1 Corinthians 15:19-23 _____

_____

_____

_____

_____

1 John 3:1-3 _____

_____

_____

_____

_____

Your inheritance through Christ
(verse 18)

Romans 8:15-17 _____

_____

_____

_____

_____

Ephesians 1:3-14 _____

_____

_____

For Further Study:
Ephesians 1:15-23 contains many rich phrases that would be fruitful to meditate on, such as "the riches of his glorious inheritance," or "his body, the fullness of him who fills everything in every way."

Choose one phrase that is especially significant to you. Meditate on it for five or ten minutes each day for the next week, and mull it over whenever you get a chance.

31

_____

_____

1 Peter 1:3-6 _____

_____

_____

_____

_____

God's power through Christ
(verses 19-23)

Romans 8:11 _____

_____

_____

_____

2 Corinthians 4:5-7, 12:9-10 _____

_____

_____

_____

John 14:12-14 _____

_____

_____

_____

_____

5. God's power in us is His power that raised Jesus
   from death, says Paul (Ephesians 1:19-20). What
   is most significant to you personally about this
   truth?

_____

_____

_____

_____

_____

_____

For Further Study: Summarize what Ephesians 1:3-23 teaches about God's power.

6. a. What knowledge (verse 17) is basic to fulfilling Paul's prayer in verses 18-19? Why?

_____

_____

_____

_____

_____

   b. What do you think are some practical means of acquiring this knowledge? (A helpful passage here might be John 14:21-26.)

_____

_____

_____

_____

_____

Right hand: (verse 20). A king's right hand symbolized his power and authority.

7. a. Describe the relationship between Christ and the Church that verses 20-23 depict.

_____

_____

_____

_____

_____

33

For Further Study: On a separate sheet of paper, write out an outline for chapter 1. You can use the partial outline on page 26 as a model for outlining 1:3-14, and then add 1:1-2 and 1:15-23 to it. (If you add to this outline as you study each passage, you will finish this study with a complete outline of Ephesians.)

Optional Application: Read the front page of a newspaper, or listen to the evening news. Think prayerfully about what you read or hear in light of what Paul prayed that the Ephesians would know. How does this knowledge affect your response to what you read or hear? Do you discover anything that you would like to pray about regularly?

b. How does Christ's position relate to you personally?

_____

_____

_____

8. In your own words, summarize 1:15-23.

_____

_____

_____

_____

_____

_____

9. List any questions you have about 1:15-23.

_____

_____

_____

_____

10. Is there one particular discovery from your study of Ephesians 1:15-23 that you would like to begin putting into practice? If so, write down what it is and how you can go about applying it.

_____

_____

_____

_____

_____

_____

_____

Following Paul's example

Begin daily to pray according to the model which Paul set forth in chapter 1 of his letter. Pray the praise, thanks, and requests for yourself and for whomever God leads you to pray, whether close to you or in distant places. (Remember how far Paul was from Ephesus.) When you meet as a group, take time to pray in this way.

For the group

Let everyone share the most significant thing he or she learned about the Christian's hope, inheritance, or power. Make sure the central teaching of the passage is clear. You might discuss what day-to-day preoccupations keep you from focusing on these truths.

The Powers of the Universe

The *rules, authorities, powers,* and *dominions* over which Paul claimed in 1:21 that Jesus had control were primarily angelic or demonic beings, who inspired much fear in Paul's day. Attempts to influence these forces created thriving industries. Every marketplace had a wizard who sold spoken charms and potions to frustrated lovers, hopeful politicians, sick people, and anyone else afraid of Fate. Ephesus was famous worldwide for its magical scrolls.

Astrology began as an exact science which sought to define the laws by which the stars influenced events on earth. Astrologists believed that one who knew the laws by which the cosmos functioned could manipulate them for the good of humans. Astrology revealed that the earth was a sphere and gave Rome the solar calendar; to this extent it was a serious science of observation, investigating a theory. However, people soon began trying to use it to predict and control the future. Cheap horoscopes were mass-produced, planetary symbols and signs of the zodiac appeared in art, coins, and jewelry, and the astrologer-for-hire set up shop next door to the wizard.

Life After Life

Philosophers taught that death was a blessed escape of the soul from the body. They held that the world of the senses was lower and transitory, while the world of the intellect, the soul, or the spirit was the true one. Philosophy appealed mainly to the educated elite, but it did manage to convince ordinary people that body and soul were separate. Most people, however, looked forward to dreary, disembodied afterlife in the underworld. Some of the mystery cults became popular by promising initiates happiness in the underworld; but no one even suggested that disgusting *bodies* might be resurrected.

1. Barth, page 148.
2. Barth, page 148.

EPHESIANS 2:1-10

Death to Life

As always, start your study by reading through 2:1-10 several times. Think about the summary you gave it on page 14 and about the letter's theme. Then read through this lesson, noting especially the subtitles.

Sin: the human condition (2:1-3)

Look at Paul's description of people who were without Christ (verse 1). He did not describe them as unfulfilled or incomplete. He said that people were *dead*; that is, their spirits were dead because they had broken relationship with the source of life: God.

Transgressions and sins: (verse 1). Milder words in Greek than Paul's usual terms denoting rebellion against God and breaking known laws of God. These suggested "lapses" or "blunders"[1] by Gentiles who did not know better or could not help themselves.

---

1. Describe in your own words the nature of the spiritually dead. Observe

   their power to do right (verse 1)

   _____

   _____

For Further Study:
How do you think a
spiritually alive person
learns what to desire
and how to obtain it?
(See Paul's prayers in
Colossians 1:9-14 and
Philippians 1:9-11.)

the primary influence on their lives (verse 2)

_____

_____

_____

_____

their main aims (verse 3)

_____

_____

_____

_____

the result of their choice of aims and masters
(verse 3)

_____

_____

_____

2. Is there any way that you fall, or have fallen in the
past, into the description of the people named in
verses 1-3? Explain.

_____

_____

_____

_____

_____

Grace: the divine solution (2:4-10)

3. Why has God saved us from the consequences of
our sin?

verse 4 _____

_____

verse 7 _____

_____

_____

_____

4. In verses 4-9, Paul tells us about some tremendous things that God has done for us. List as many as you can find, and try to put them in your own words—rather than using the actual phrases Paul selects.

_____

_____

_____

_____

_____

_____

_____

5. According to verses 8-9, what is our part in responding to what God has done?

_____

_____

_____

_____

Works: what for?

6. a. What is our nature and purpose, according to verse 10?

_____

_____

_____

_____

For Thought and Discussion: Pagans in Ephesus tried to remove guilt by maiming themselves, abstaining from food or sex, giving money, or sacrificing an animal. How do people in your day try to remove guilt, other than by accepting God's grace?

For Thought and Discussion: Review your answer to question 4 on this page. How might your findings help you comprehend and respond to what Paul means by "the incomparable riches of his grace"?

For Further Study:
Cross-referencing should follow a logical process to assure that you are seeing statements in context. Compare other references to *grace* first in Ephesians, next in Paul's other letters, then elsewhere in the New Testament, and finally in the Old Testament. Consult at least five cross-references, adding others depending upon how far you wish to pursue your study. (Look up *grace* and *gracious* in a concordance.)

b. Verses 8-9 explain that saving faith is a gift from God. If our good works will not earn for us God's love, nearness, or blessing, what does their purpose seem to be (1:12, 2:10)? (*Optional:* See also Matthew 5:16, John 15:8, Titus 3:8.)

_____

_____

_____

_____

_____

_____

_____

7. List three ways in which you can find out which works God has "prepared in advance" for you, as opposed to those you are doing to make yourself feel good, to earn love, etc.

James 1:5-8 _____

_____

2 Timothy 3:16-17 _____

_____

John 15:5,10 _____

_____

8. Sum up the central teaching of 2:1-10 in a sentence.

_____

_____

_____

_____

_____

_____

_____

9. How do you think 2:1-10 relates to chapter 1?

_____

_____

_____

_____

_____

Your response

10. Read Matthew 25:31-46 and 28:18-20. Write down anything you find in these two passages that you think are some of the "good works" God has prepared for you to do.

_____

_____

_____

_____

_____

_____

_____

Workmanship: (verse 10). A "work of art,"[2] not a common thing.

11. List any questions you have about 2:1-10.

_____

_____

_____

_____

_____

For Further Study:
Make up an outline of this passage that will be helpful in grasping the major points, their sequence, and their relationship to each other.

For Further Study:
Compare references to good works in Paul's other letters, in the rest of the New Testament, in the Old Testament.

Optional Application: How does knowing that you are God's "workmanship" affect the way you feel about yourself? How does it affect the way you perceive your purpose in living?

Optional Application: Write out the verse(s) in this passage that spoke most deeply to you. Try memorizing them in a version you find helpful.

12. Have you had any insight from 2:1-10 that you would like to focus on during the next week? If so, write down what seems important to you and how you might respond to it.

_____

_____

_____

_____

_____

_____

_____

Are you, as an individual or in teamwork with a group, still working at praise, thanksgiving, and petition? How are you doing?

For the group

Look for ways of encouraging each other to grow in awareness of what it means (practically) to be God's workmanship.

Make sure everyone understands a) what it means to be spiritually dead and alive; b) how that change is possible; and c) why we do good works.

1. Barth, pages 83-84. See also "Trespass" in W.E. Vine, *An Expository Dictionary of New Testament Words* (Nashville: Royal Publishers, Inc., 1952), page 1166.
2. Barth, page 226.

LESSON FIVE

EPHESIANS 2:11-22

Peace

"In the first part of chapter 2, Paul said that in Christ we become new men morally and spiritually. Here he says that in Christ we become new men religiously and culturally."[1]

Read 2:11-22 slowly twice. Recall what the whole passage is about and how it relates to the letter's theme.

Before Christ: enemies

Gentiles: (verse 11). Literally, "nations," or "ethnic groups," a somewhat contemptuous term for non-Jews. "Uncircumcised" was a very contemptuous term.

Circumcision: (verse 11). A ritual cutting away of the foreskin, signifying that a man is a Jew. Paul liked to quote Moses' and Jeremiah's teaching that true circumcision is "circumcision of the heart"—that is, obedience in faith (Romans 2:28-29; compare Deuteronomy 10:16, Jeremiah 4:4).

The five descriptions of the Gentiles' position in Ephesians 2:12 are roughly synonyms: before Christ, only Jews were among the community of those with whom

43

For Further Study:
Find out what each of
the Old Testament
"covenants of the
promise" was.

For Further Study:
Who is the "one new
man" of verse 15?
(What else does Paul
say about him in
Ephesians?)

God had begun a relationship through "covenants of
the promise." These covenants included all the Old
Testament contracts based upon God's promises—with
Noah, Abraham, Isaac, Jacob, Moses, David, Judah,
and Levi. In particular, the promise of the Messiah had
been given only to Israel, although the prophets had
hinted that non-Hebrews would be included (see, for
example, Isaiah 55:3-5). Because of the promises, Jews
had been "near" to God and His Messiah, but Gentiles
had been "far away."

1. a. Paraphrase Ephesians 2:12—what was the non-
Jews' relationship to God and His promises
before Christ?

_____

_____

_____

_____

_____

b. Paraphrase verse 13—what is their new relationship, and how has it been established?

_____

_____

_____

_____

_____

2. What was the "barrier" (verse 14) between Gentiles and Jews before Christ (verses 12-15)?

_____

_____

_____

_____

_____

Law with its commandments and regulations (verse 15). Not the eternal moral and physical principles by which God's creation runs, but rather a) the ceremonial rules of the Law of Moses or b) the scribes' elaborations on the Law.

In Christ: reconciled

3. How did Jesus reconcile Jews and Gentiles; that is, how did He break the barrier between them (verses 14-16)?

_____

_____

_____

_____

_____

_____

4. What do you think is the "peace" that Jesus preached (verse 17; compare verse 14)?

_____

_____

_____

_____

5. What result of Christ's work does verse 18 describe?

_____

_____

_____

_____

For Further Study:
Verse 14 says "for he himself is our peace." How is Christ our peace? What does this mean? (Study how Paul used the word in this context. Look at the definition on page 17, or find another in a Bible dictionary. Find in a concordance other places where Paul used the word. Does it mean the same here as in Romans 5:1?)

6. It seems that the *reason* for the change in human relationships touches the core of the letter: Paul's vision of what the Church is supposed to be. He described the Church in a series of images. Name each image and tell what it teaches you about how Christians are supposed to function together.

Image	What it teaches about human relationships
(2:15-16; 1:22-23)	
(2:19)	
(2:20-22)	

Prophets (verse 20). Probably refers not just to the Old Testament prophets but also to those in the early Church recognized as having the spiritual gifts of speaking God's word for the immediate situation and of seeing future events as present (Acts 11:27-28, 13:1).

For Further Study:
Add to your outline of Ephesians by outlining 2:11-22.

7. State in a sentence the main teaching of 2:11-22.

_____

_____

_____

_____

_____

8. How does this passage relate to 2:1-10? (Notice the connectors "therefore" in verse 11 and "consequently" in verse 19.)

_____

_____

_____

_____

_____

_____

9. What does Paul's argument so far have to do with his purposes for writing this letter? How does chapter 1 serve those purposes? Chapter 2?

_____

_____

_____

_____

_____

_____

Optional Applica-
tion: Choose a key
verse or verses from
2:11-22 to memorize
and meditate on this
week.

10. Read over your responses to the questions in this lesson. Seek God's guidance through prayer to choose at least one change in your attitudes toward other Christians. Pray for His grace to change your behavior, and then record the specific first steps you can take to begin bringing this area of your life into conformity with His will.

_____

_____

_____

_____

_____

_____

_____

11. List any questions you have about 2:11-22.

_____

_____

_____

_____

_____

For the group

Make sure that everyone understands how Christ has made us one. See that Paul's images make sense.

Give members a chance to share any questions they have about the passage. If no one can answer them, map out a plan for finding the answers.

Pray together for relations among churches in your neighborhood and throughout the world.

How can your group work at resembling Paul's images of the Church?

Church Factions in Ephesus?

In the 40's and 50's AD, Christianity was still seen as a sect of Judaism. Jewish Christians in many cities considered themselves the superior members of the Church, and believers bickered over whether Gentiles had to become Jews in order to be Christians. Paul had to explain the doctrine of justification by faith in order to restore unity. In defending the status of the Gentiles, he sternly criticized his Jewish kinsmen who were burdening fellow Christians.

A decade later, however, the Asian churches were filling with Gentiles who were less familiar with Judaism than "God-fearers" were, and who knew only of justification by faith and of Paul's harsh words for Jews. These Gentiles may have begun to question whether Jews who still respected the Law of Moses could belong to the Church. Instead of writing a biting rhetorical epistle as he had to Galatia, the aging Paul chose to share his vision of the Church in the form of a prayer—the letter to the Ephesians. As always, his aim was for the people to know who they were *in Christ*—His Body—and to live out that identity. The appeal for unity was the same; no faction was to consider itself more holy than another.

1. Tom Julien, *Inherited Wealth: Studies in Ephesians,* (Winona Lake, Indiana: BMH Books, 1976), page 43.

EPHESIANS 3:1-13

Paul's Mission

Read 3:1-13 a couple of times.

Paul began this section with "For this reason" in verse 1 but inserted a long parenthesis in verses 2 through 13. Thus, the "For this reason" in verse 14 picks up again where Paul broke off in verse 1.

Mystery: (verse 3). A secret. Unlike the guarded rites of the mystery cults and the close-kept knowledge of the gnostics (see pages 58 and 64), there was nothing "mysterious" or incomprehensible about God's secret. It was simply kept until God chose to reveal it, and now it is absolutely not to be kept private.

1. a. Read verses 1-2 and 7-8. What was Paul's attitude toward his ministry?

   _____

   _____

   _____

   _____

   _____

   _____

   _____

b. What does his attitude teach about service to God?

_____

_____

_____

_____

_____

_____

2. a. In verse 3, Paul speaks of the "mystery" that God made known to him. What is this mystery (verses 3-6)?

_____

_____

_____

_____

_____

_____

b. Why do you think Paul describes it the way he does in verse 8?

_____

_____

_____

_____

_____

_____

3. a. What was God's timetable for revealing this mystery (verses 5,9-10)?

_____

_____

_____

_____

_____

b. What was God's purpose in this plan (verses 10-11)?

_____

_____

_____

_____

_____

_____

For Thought and Discussion: From 2:11-22, why do you think the mystery of Christ might have surprised the Jews?

4. Define what you think Paul meant by "grace" in verse 2 and verses 7-8. Compare your answers to the definition on page 17.

verse 2 _____

_____

_____

_____

_____

verses 7-8 _____

_____

_____

_____

_____

_____

Freedom: (verse 12). A legal right: freedom to speak frankly or to stand without fear, especially before a ruler.[1] "Boldness" in most other versions.

53

For Further Study:
What other attitudes
does the Bible teach
about approaching
God? (Include specific
references in your
answer.)

5. a. What does verse 12 teach about conditions and
attitudes in seeking God?

_____

_____

_____

_____

_____

   b. What are some practical implications of this
verse?

_____

_____

_____

_____

_____

Discouraged: (verse 13). "To become tired, lazy, de-
spondent, and desperate,"[2] or to lose strength.

---

6. Explain in your own words what our "freedom and
confidence" in approaching God (verse 12) is
founded on.

_____

_____

_____

_____

_____

For Further Study:
Make up your own out-
line of 3:1-13, one
which highlights the
passage's main points.

Glory: (verse 13). "The honour resulting from a good opinion."[3] When used of God, it also has the Old Testament meaning of His spiritual radiance which reflects His praiseworthiness. (See Ephesians 1:6,12,14.)

7 a. Read 1 Corinthians 4:9-13 and 2 Corinthians 11:24-29, and summarize the suffering to which Paul referred in Ephesians 3:13.

_____

_____

_____

_____

b. To earn this suffering, all Paul had done was to preach the gospel (Ephesians 3:8). What kinds of suffering are not glorious (1 Peter 2:19-23, 4:15-16)?

_____

_____

_____

_____

c. Describe Paul's attitude about his suffering (verse 13).

_____

_____

_____

8. What do you think is the main message of 3:1-13?

_____

_____

_____

_____

55

9. Why do you think Paul inserted this parenthesis (verses 2-13) justifying his authority and explaining his mission? Think about the purpose of the letter and the opinion his readers might have had of him.

_____

_____

_____

_____

_____

_____

10. Has there been a particular insight from this lesson that you would like to focus on in the next week? You might want to write it down here, so that it doesn't slip out of your thoughts when you go on to the next section. Pray for God's leading in ways to make this truth or principle really take hold in your life.

_____

_____

_____

_____

_____

_____

11. List any questions you have about this passage.

_____

_____

_____

_____

_____

For the group

You may want to focus your discussion on one or two of the issues this passage raises. For instance:

Mission (What was Paul's mission? What might yours be? How can you find out? What makes a person hesitate to identify and pursue his mission?)

Suffering (How can you acquire Paul's attitude toward suffering in mission?)

The mystery of Christ (Why was the salvation of the Gentiles a "mystery"? How might it be significant for you? How did Christ make it possible? What are the "unsearchable riches" and the "promise" of Christ?)

Share with one another how you are progressing in the changes for which you have been praying and working since you began this study. Rededicate yourselves, continue to pray for one another, and seek ways to "spur one another on toward love and good deeds" (Hebrews 10:24). What can you do to help one another grow?

The Missionary

The Book of Acts says that Paul rented a hall in Ephesus in which to give regular public lectures. This was a common practice of teachers in the Empire. The ease of travel brought a steady stream of wandering teachers through the Asian cities, each promising skills for success, the secret of the good life, or the worship of the true god. Some arrived with an idol on a litter, others wore outlandish costumes, and still others came in the simple robe, beard, and sandals of the traditional philosopher. Some prophesied ecstatically, others gave loud, stirring speeches, and others taught quietly and learnedly. Many performed miraculous signs and healings.

People loved to hear new things, but a traveling missionary had to overcome the smugness of city people who had heard it all before. They wanted to be entertained or to escape their daily lives, but they were used to experimenting with a new philosophy or cult whenever an old one lost its freshness.

"Mystery" Cults

Private cult societies touched most Ephesians much more deeply than did the public gods. Some societies were simply clubs attached to a public temple; a group of men or several families might own a room connected to the temple in which they would hold ceremonial meals after a liturgy (worship service). Some were connected with the industrial guilds, since most guilds had patron deities. But increasingly popular were the "mystery" religions, cults with regular meetings which only members who had undergone initiation might attend.

Meetings included ritual meals and ceremonies, and members were often subject to strict moral codes, the stern discipline of a leader, and bizarre traditions. Ascetic restraints on food and sex were common, as were rules of ritual cleanliness. Breaking a taboo incurred the wrath of the god and required penance in the form of an offering or some punishment. (Asceticism and penance were not limited to mystery cults, however, for most people believed that the human body was a prison in which the true person, the soul, longed for escape. Religions varied in their degree of distaste for anything physical.)

Initiation usually involved participation in a ritual drama, in which the initiate symbolically died and was remade by the god, or became "immortal." The rite gave "saving" power for a limited time; people often repeated the ceremony or were initiated into several cults, for none demanded exclusive loyalty.

Initiation was open to anyone regardless of social class or even gender, for the cults were meant to allow temporary escape from social roles. However, since initiation was usually expensive, only the few with money or a patron could afford it. Contact with the divine was a luxury.

1. Barth, page 330.
2. Barth, page 349.
3. "Glory" in Vine, page 483.

EPHESIANS 3:14-21

Prayer for Power

Read through the passage first, and review the letter's theme.

1. After reminding his hearers of their former condition, of God's past and continuing transformation of them, and of his own mission, Paul began to describe a prayer in 3:14-21. Why do you think the truths of chapter 2 led to this particular prayer? (Recall that the "for this reason" in 3:14 is a restatement of the phrase in 3:1.)

_____

_____

_____

_____

_____

_____

Family: (verse 15). Human clans and angelic orders; possibly also local churches.

Name: (verse 15). "Identity, essence, function."[1] Also, Jews held that the giver of the name held authority over the thing named.

2. What do verses 14 and 15 teach about

   a. Paul's attitude toward God?

   _____

   _____

   _____

   _____

   _____

   _____

   _____

   b. God's sovereignty?

   _____

   _____

   _____

   _____

   _____

   _____

   _____

Inner being: (verse 16). That part of the believer which was made alive (2:5; compare Romans 7:22 and 2 Corinthians 4:16) but which may still be weak or asleep (Ephesians 5:14). A newly reborn person is a baby (1 Corinthians 3:1-3, 1 Peter 2:2, Hebrews 5:13-14).

3. Look carefully at Paul's prayer for the Ephesians in 3:16-19. In the chart on the next page, write in the lefthand column each of the specific requests that Paul prayed for the Ephesians. Then, in the righthand column, put Paul's request into your own words by paraphrasing it as a prayer for yourself.

What Paul prayed for the Ephesians	What I need to ask God for in my life

For Further Study: How is a Christian "rooted and established in love" (verse 17)? Think about chapters 1-2.

For Thought and Discussion: Take a look at verse 19. How can you know something that surpasses knowledge? What do you think Paul meant?

4. What seems to be Paul's emphasis in this prayer?

_____

_____

_____

_____

_____

For Further Study:
What does it mean to
be filled with God's fullness (verse 19)? Study
other references to full-
ness and filling in
Ephesians, and then in
others of Paul's letters.

**For Thought and Dis-
cussion:** What does
Paul's praise of God in
verses 20-21 have to
do with the rest of this
passage? If verse 20 is
true, why does it some-
times seem that God
is inactive in the world,
the Church, a life?
(See, for instance,
John 14:21 or Isaiah
59:1-11.)

5. Notice that Paul shifts his emphasis somewhat in
   verses 20-21, as he closes his prayer. What do
   these two verses teach you about

   God? _____

   _____

   _____

   _____

   your relationship to Him? _____

   _____

   _____

   _____

   _____

   _____

   _____

   God's purposes for all believers? _____

   _____

   _____

   _____

   _____

6. Write out what you now believe is the main teaching of 3:14-21.

   _____

   _____

   _____

   _____

   _____

7. How does this passage relate to chapters 1 and 2, and to the purposes of the letter?

_____

_____

_____

_____

_____

_____

For Further Study:
Even if you have not been working on an outline of Ephesians, try outlining 3:14-21.

Optional Application: Memorize Paul's prayer in verses 16-19. Pray it daily for yourself and others. Or, meditate on the praise in verses 20-21.

8. What truth about God's love discussed in chapters 1-3 seems most significant to you today? Why?

_____

_____

_____

_____

_____

_____

9. List any questions you have about 3:14-21.

_____

_____

_____

_____

For the group

Add prayer for power to your prayers for one another and for the whole Church.

How can you help one another within your group to use the gifts of power and love?

"I tell you the truth, anyone who has faith in me will do what I have been doing. He will do even greater things than these, because I am going to the Father." (John 14:12)

Knowledge

Knowledge was power in the Roman Empire. Everybody wanted it; many claimed to have it. Astrologists claimed knowledge to control the stars which governed fate, cults offered the secrets of rites to gain prosperity in life and death, and philosophies taught the "how-to's" of a satisfying life.

One understanding of knowledge that was just being formed is called *Gnosticism*, from *gnosis*, the Greek word for knowledge. To the Gnostic, the world was the disastrous result of an upheaval within the deity. The human soul was part of the divine somehow caught in an evil and alien world. Salvation would be the end of the world, when souls could escape. The only way to live in the world was to "know" that one was a foreigner and to ignore the world. Then it could not control you.

Different Gnostics believed that different revealers had come from outside the world to "awaken" them from their "drunken stupor" by informing them of the secret knowledge. "Knowledge" was not understanding of a series of doctrines, nor relationship with a person, but rather recognition of the truth about oneself and the world. It was not something to be noised around to everyone; it was a "mystery," a secret jealously guarded from the corrupt masses.

Paul showed in his letter some familiarity with words Gnostics liked, such as *mystery* and *knowledge*, but he seems to have used them almost deliberately in ungnostic ways. He used language familiar to his readers in order to stress the differences between the gospel and competing beliefs.

1. Barth, page 383.

EPHESIANS 4:1-16

Unity Lived Out

Commands

Calling: (verse 1). Suggests a high and honorable state.

1. Paul began chapter 4 with *Therefore* ("then" in NIV). This connecting word is a clue to how all that follows relates to all that has gone before. What does 4:1 lead you to expect in chapters 4-6?

_____

_____

_____

_____

2. From what you learned in chapters 1-3, what do you think Paul wants you to remember about the "calling" we have received?

_____

_____

_____

_____

3. Read the character qualities Paul urges us to take on in 4:2. How can these traits help us fulfill the command in 4:3?

_____

_____

_____

_____

_____

_____

As you consider the meanings of the traits and attitudes Paul described, note that Paul urged these traits and attitudes with full certainty that his audience had the power (3:16-21) to live up to his standard. Note also that he rarely urged them to *do* certain things, but usually to *be* a certain way.

Humble: (verse 2; KJV: "lowliness"). Willing to take little honor or to give higher place to another. In pagan eyes humility suggested the cringing of a slave or lack of self-respect. (Mark 10:42-44, Luke 14:7-11, John 13:3-14, Romans 12:3-10, 1 Peter 5:5-6.)

Gentle: (verse 2; KJV: "meekness"). Having no one to turn to except God or a benevolent king, so that one accepts His treatment without resistance or bitterness. Gentleness also was no virtue to the Greeks, who believed in using might for right, but Judaism honored Moses as meek. (Numbers 12:3, Matthew 5:5.)

Patient: (verse 2; KJV: "longsuffering"). "Having a wide . . . soul"[1] so that one can bear with the burdensome neighbor; "self-restraint in the face of provocation."[2] (Matthew 18:21-35, Romans 12:19-21.)

66

4. a. What is the central, unifying point of Paul's declaration in Ephesians 4:4-6?

_____

_____

_____

_____

_____

  b. What light does this declaration shed on verses 1-3, if at all?

_____

_____

_____

_____

_____

_____

For Further Study:
Any of these words ("humble," "gentle," "patient") would make a good word study. Study how one of them is used elsewhere in the New Testament. Or, read through a Gospel, and notice how Jesus exemplified these traits.

Why Christians differ

Having emphasized the unity among believers, Paul seems to move on in verses 7 through 16 to explain how and why Christians differ.

_____

When he ascended . . . to men: (verse 8). Compare Psalm 68:18. Jews sang Psalm 68 in their synagogues on Pentecost (the Feast of Weeks), the day on which they thanked God for His providence of all goods under the terms of the covenant. The psalm exalts God as a conqueror returning to His capitol in triumph.

The last line of verse 18 reads in Hebrew, "you received gifts from men." Most commentators think that Paul either himself inverted the words to stress that Christ is much more the giver than the receiver of gifts, or was quoting a Christian hymn which had changed the psalm to make the same point.[3]

_____

Descended: (verse 9). Some believe Paul meant that Christ descended to the underworld "to preach the gospel to those who had died before His coming." Others think he meant that Christ descended to the lowest state in the universe, not just living on earth as a human, but even going down to death and the place of death as a human. Compare Philippians 2:8.[4]

5. a. What do you think is the "grace" Christ has given to each believer (verse 7)? See Ephesians 4:12, Romans 12:4-6.

_____

_____

_____

_____

_____

  b. Why do you think Paul immediately followed this statement with the explanations in Ephesians 4:8-9?

_____

_____

_____

_____

_____

_____

Apostles, . . . prophets, . . . evangelists, . . . pastors and teachers: (verse 11). All "Ministers of the Word."[5] An "evangelist" was a missionary of lower authority than an apostle, who brought the gospel into new regions. A "pastor" (literally, "shepherd") was probably a local overseer of a church, also called a "bishop." (See page 16 on "apostles" and page 47 on "prophets.")

6. According to verses 11-13, what else has Christ given us, and for what purpose?

_____

_____

_____

_____

_____

Optional Application: What equipping for "works of service" do you think you most need right now?
    How could you seek it?

7. What is our unity *in* (verse 13), and what are some practical implications for your own life?

_____

_____

_____

_____

_____

_____

_____

_____

Mature: (verse 13). Literally, "a mature man." Suggests not just that every individual Christian is to be mature, but also that God's goal is to knit the individuals together into "one new man" (2:15)—Christ.

8. What are the chief signs of spiritual maturity (verses 13-15) and immaturity (verse 14) in the faith?

maturity _____

_____

_____

_____

_____

For Further Study:
Study more of Paul's teaching on the purpose of spiritual gifts in 1 Corinthians 12.

immaturity _____

_____

_____

_____

_____

9. a. What do you think it means to speak the truth in love (verse 15)?

_____

_____

_____

_____

_____

_____

b. Can you offer an example of speaking the truth that is *not* done in love?

_____

_____

_____

_____

_____

_____

10. Look again at Paul's metaphor (image, picture, analogy) for the Church in verses 15-16. What does this description suggest to you about

your own spiritual growth?

_____

_____

_____

_____

the collective growth of all believers in the Body of Christ?

_____

_____

_____

_____

_____

11. State what you think is the main teaching of 4:1-16.

_____

_____

_____

_____

_____

_____

For Further Study: Paul structured this passage very carefully, so you may find that an outline will help you to understand 4:1-16. Notice how Paul holds unity and diversity together.

Optional Application: What is one practical way you can contribute to the unity Paul urges us toward in this passage?

Your response

12. Is there a particular insight you have gained from this lesson that you would like to concentrate on in your own life? If so, write down what it is and how you could begin working on it.

_____

_____

_____

_____

_____

_____

_____

13. List any questions you have about 4:1-16.

_____

_____

_____

_____

For the group

Try to focus on one or two concepts that seem key to your group.

Be sure to let members ask questions about the passage. You might assign someone to seek answers for your next meeting.

Your small group is an excellent place in which to practice the traits discussed in this passage. Discuss in your group how you can help one another.

1. Barth, *Ephesians 4-6*, Anchor Bible, Volume 34A, (Garden City, New York: Doubleday and Company, Inc., 1974), page 459.
2. Vine, page 840.
3. Francis Foulkes, *The Epistle of Paul to the Ephesians*, Tyndale New Testament Commentaries, (Grand Rapids, Michigan: William B. Eerdmans Publishing Company, 1981), page 115.
4. Foulkes, page 116.
5. Barth, page 436.

EPHESIANS 4:17-32

Put Off . . . Put On

Read this passage carefully a couple of times, noting its main points and recalling 4:1.

A profile of sinners

1. In verses 17-19, Paul describes how the ungodly live. What are the chief characteristics he ascribes to them?

_____

_____

_____

_____

_____

_____

_____

_____

Sensuality: (verse 19). Lewdness; implies sexual depravity, violence, a refusal to recognize limits. Paul may have associated it with the ritual prostitution and other practices at the temple of Artemis-Cybele in Ephesus.

2. What do you think hardness of heart (verse 18) is?
(See Hebrews 3:7-13.)

_____

_____

_____

_____

_____

3. Why do you think Paul insists so emphatically in
verse 17?

_____

_____

_____

_____

_____

4. Do you think there are any warnings here for
Christians? If so, what might they be?

_____

_____

_____

_____

_____

_____

The new life in Christ

_____

Corruption: (verse 22). Literally, "rotting," decaying
as a dying or dead thing.[1]

_____

5. Study Paul's summary of what the Ephesians had
been taught about life in Christ (verses 20-24). In

74

the following chart, write in the appropriate columns 1) the three things the Ephesians had been taught to do, and 2) how you could put each teaching into practice.

What the Ephesians were taught	How I could put it into practice
verse 22	
verse 23	
verse 24	

6. Do you think Paul intended these as three separate steps? Why or why not?

_____

_____

_____

_____

_____

_____

7. Look up Romans 8:5-6 and Romans 12:1-2. Write down anything you find that helps to shed light on the process Paul describes in Ephesians 4:22-24.

_____

_____

_____

_____

_____

Specific instructions

8. In verses 25-32, Paul lists some specific rules for living in "true righteousness and holiness" (verse 24). What are the commands Paul gives in verses 25-28?

_____

_____

_____

_____

_____

_____

9. Read Matthew 12:33-37. How might Jesus' insight help us to understand why Paul commanded Ephesians 4:22-24 before 4:25-32?

_____

_____

_____

_____

_____

_____

_____

For Further Study:
Look up James 3:1-4:3 and 4:11-12 as an illuminating cross-reference to Ephesians 4:25-27. What can you find in James' teaching that sheds light on 1) Paul's reference to speaking truthfully, and 2) the causes and solutions to anger?

10. Can you find any clues in 4:25-28 as to *why* Paul gave this command? Think in terms of the kind of perspective on life Paul wanted the Ephesians to have.

_____

_____

_____

_____

_____

_____

11. a. Look again at verses 26-27. Why do you think Paul was anxious to get this point across?

_____

_____

_____

_____

_____

_____

For Thought and Discussion: What are some specific examples of the kinds of speech Paul is 1) warning us away from, and 2) urging us toward in Ephesians 4:29?

b. What are some possible ways to obey this particular command? (Try to be specific in your answer.)

_____

_____

_____

_____

_____

_____

_____

12. a. What seems to be Paul's purpose behind the command he gives in 4:29?

_____

_____

_____

_____

_____

b. Do you think this command has any relationship to the one in 4:25? Why or why not?

_____

_____

_____

_____

_____

_____

13. a. In 4:30, Paul tells us not to "grieve the Holy Spirit." How do the following two verses (31-32)

explain what Paul meant by an offense to God's Spirit?

_____

_____

_____

_____

_____

_____

_____

b. What does the possibility of grieving the Holy Spirit tell you about the nature of this Person of the Trinity?

_____

_____

_____

_____

_____

14. Why do you think Paul reminded his readers that they had been "sealed for the day of redemption" (verse 30) by the Holy Spirit?

_____

_____

_____

_____

_____

15. a. What is the model for forgiveness set before us in verse 32?

_____

_____

_____

b. Why is this model important to our relationships with others?

_____

_____

_____

_____

_____

16. a. Write down the character qualities Paul lists in verse 32.

_____

_____

_____

_____

b. How could you practically demonstrate these qualities in your own life? For your answer, apply the qualities to the behavior Paul teaches in verses 25-29.

_____

_____

_____

_____

_____

_____

_____

_____

17. Is there any area of your thought or behavior that you have been convicted of in your study of Ephesians 4:17-32? If so, write it down, as well as some steps that you could begin to take this week (talk to God; ask a friend to pray for you and help you;

begin establishing a habit, etc.) in order to put your desire for obedience into action.

For Further Study: Make up an outline for 4:17-32.

Optional Application: Memorize and meditate on any verses from this passage that you believe God is using right now to help you conform to His image.

_____

_____

_____

_____

_____

_____

_____

18. a. Summarize what you believe to be the main teaching of 4:17-32.

_____

_____

_____

_____

_____

b. How does it relate to 4:1-16?

_____

_____

_____

_____

_____

19. List any questions you have about 4:17-32.

_____

_____

_____

_____

_____

_____

For the group

This is a long lesson. You might want to focus your
discussion on the motives Paul gives for action, and
on how a Christian goes about acquiring the godly
traits Paul names. How does 4:22-24 work in practice?
Then share how you intend to apply these verses to
yourselves.

Be sure to let members ask questions about anything that seems unclear. Cross-references from a concordance or reference Bible may help.

Galatians 6:2 urges us to bear one another's
burdens. As each person shares his or her struggles
with the traits of 4:25-32, look for ways to help and
encourage one another.

1. Barth, page 502.

EPHESIANS 5:1-20

Imitating God

Having said in chapters 1-3 that salvation—reconciliation with God—is God's unearned gift, Paul went
on to give his audience reasons to live ethically and a
description of what ethical life is. Read 5:1-20 several
times.

1. a. What do you think is the major reason for
ethical living that Paul gave in chapters 1
through 4?

_____

_____

_____

_____

_____

  b. For some specific aspects of this reason, consult
the following passages from Ephesians:

  2:4-5 _____

  _____

  2:10 _____

  _____

  2:19 _____

  _____

4:1 _____

_____

4:30 _____

_____

2. Now, what reasons does 5:1-20 add?

5:2 _____

_____

5:5-6 _____

_____

5:8 _____

_____

5:11 _____

_____

5:15-16 _____

_____

3. a. Look carefully at 5:1-2. What does Paul tell the Ephesians to do?

_____

_____

_____

b. What does the context (verses 1-2) of Paul's command suggest to you about what following this instruction means?

_____

_____

_____

_____

_____

_____

4. a. What kinds of purposes and goals in life do you
      think would be necessary in order to obey
      Paul's command to "live a life of love" (verse 2)?

   _____

   _____

   _____

   _____

   _____

   _____

   b. Can you think of some examples of practical
      acts of love toward those outside your family?
      What might they be?

   _____

   _____

   _____

   _____

   _____

   _____

5. Read the kinds of behavior that Paul denounces in
   verses 3-4. Is there anything here that sounds a
   warning to you? What kinds of thoughts or
   actions should you be on your guard against?

   _____

   _____

   _____

   _____

   _____

For Thought and Discussion: Verses 5-6 may seem to imply that no one who sins through immorality, impurity, or greed can be saved. How do 1 John 1:9-10, 3:6 and Romans 8:1-5 shed light on these verses?

Immorality: (verse 3). The Greek word *porneia* (from which we get *pornography*), which meant illicit sexual relations.

---

6. Why do you think Paul called an immoral, impure, or covetous person an idolater (verse 5)? How are these sins idolatrous?

_____

_____

_____

_____

_____

7. What do you think Paul means in Ephesians 5:7 by warning us not to become "partners" with those who are disobedient?

_____

_____

_____

_____

_____

8. Trace the characteristics of light and darkness in verses 8-14.

Light	Darkness

9. How would you explain what it means to "live as children of light" (verse 8)?

_____

_____

_____

_____

_____

For Further Study: Study uses of the "light" image elsewhere in the New Testament. Look at Paul's other letters, at Jesus' words in the Gospels, at 1 John. If you like, look next at Old Testament references.

Find out: (verse 10). By experience, not just by hearsay.
_____

Expose: (verse 11). Prove them fruitless, probably by conduct, less probably by private or public scolding.

10. To Christians struggling with unholy habits, what counsel did Paul give?

verses 10,17 _____

_____

verse 11 _____

_____

Foolish: (verse 17). Used "to describe an inert object, a statue, or a crazed, frantic, silly or foolish person."[1] May include hard-heartedness and panicked or compulsive behavior.

11. a. Read 5:15-17. Why do you think Paul inserted this advice?

_____

_____

87

For Further Study: In verse 18, Paul commanded his readers to "be filled with the Spirit." Study the following cross-references, and record what each teaches about who the Spirit is, how you become filled with Him, and what the effects of that filling are. (Note: the verb *be filled* implies continual, habitual practice.) Luke 11:13, John 14:15-17, John 14:26, Acts 1:8, Acts 4:7-13, Romans 8:2-4, Romans 8:5-14, Ephesians 3:16.

For Thought and Discussion: Paul contrasted being "drunk on wine" with being "filled with the Spirit" (verse 18). The Jews who witnessed the Spirit's first descent at Pentecost noticed similarities between the two states (Acts 2:13). Think about how alcohol affects a drunk person. How is being filled with the Spirit like, but also opposite to, being drunk? (See also Romans 8:5-14.)

_____

_____

_____

b. List every practical implication you can think of that this instruction suggests for setting personal direction in life.

_____

_____

_____

_____

_____

_____

12. Why do you think Paul commanded his readers to "be filled with the Spirit" (verse 18)?

_____

_____

_____

_____

_____

_____

13. What does 5:19-20 teach about

our relationship to God? _____

_____

_____

_____

our relationships with others? _____

_____

_____

_____

our responses to circumstances? _____

_____

_____

_____

_____

14. Is there anything you think God is leading you to concentrate on that came up in your study of 5:1-20? How could you go about finding out what pleases the Lord in this area?

_____

_____

_____

_____

_____

_____

15. Summarize what seems to be the central teaching of 5:1-20.

_____

_____

_____

_____

_____

16. List any questions you have about this passage.

_____

_____

_____

_____

_____

Optional Applica-tion: Take time today to pray about whether you may be trying to keep any area of your life in darkness (verses 8-14)—that is, not trying to find out what is pleasing to the Lord in that area. (Since there may be some sin you're not even aware of, ask God to convict you of anything you're doing that is displeasing to Him. Prayer and counsel with other Christians can be very useful here.)

For Further Study: Try outlining 5:1-20, even if you have not been keeping an outline so far.

The Cost of Conversion

Most Ephesians considered Jews and Christians to be "haters of humanity"—antisocial. They refused to participate in any of the many festivals, games, and theatrical shows, for these civic events were usually in honor of some god and often included sacrifices. When the whole town turned out to celebrate the anniversary of a temple with food and drink, dancing and flowers, Jews and Christians stayed home. Furthermore, they would not eat with normal folk because all the meat came from temple butchers. They also liked to meet in small, private groups where "who knew what" went on. Jews were tolerated because they merely followed the religion of their ancestors, but conversion was a shocking sin which ordinary cults did not require.

A man with ambition could go only so far in sympathy with religions like these. No one who would not offer incense to the emperor's guardian, say a blessing over a civic sacrifice, or contribute money for a temple could hold public office. A meeting at one's trade association almost always included a rite for its patron god. And one could scarcely do business with a man while refusing to eat with him.

In short, conversion meant rejecting family, friends, business associates, and a whole way of life. It was not undertaken lightly.

1. Barth, page 579.

EPHESIANS 5:21-33

Submission 1

Submit: (verses 21,22). The command to "subordinate oneself"[1] was a command to a person with free choice to place himself in a position not ordained by nature. It meant "a voluntary attitude of giving in, cooperating, assuming responsibility, and carrying a burden."[2] It was usually a military term denoting the place in the ranks each division was to take. Greeks and Jews almost never used it to describe marriage.

This passage can best be understood in light of social relations in the Roman Empire. Husbands were the undisputed masters of their wives, parents of children, and owners of slaves. Thus, the command for submission to superiors was directed at people who in secular terms had no real option other than acceptance of their positions. Subordinates were simply to change the attitudes with which they regarded their situations.

On the other hand, Paul meant his commands to those in authority to be as binding as the duties of those who had no choice but to obey. Far from simply sanctioning power relationships, he meant to put them in the perspective of the primary relationship—that of each person and of the whole Church to Christ.

Paul wanted to counter the fear that Christian ethics of equality would destroy the social order. He believed that the order could serve a useful, sanctifying purpose, and he did not want to become embroiled in changing it until the hearts of individuals were transformed. Paul seems to have felt that *any* relationship would be abusive if a self-centered person was in it seeking control, whereas *any* relationship, no matter how outwardly authoritarian, would benefit both persons if each had Christ's lordship and the other person's highest good at heart.

1. Verse 21 describes the general attitude that Christians should have toward one another, regardless of rank. Name that attitude, and write down some defining words or phrases to help you think about this concept.

   _____

   _____

   _____

   _____

   _____

   _____

Reverence: (verse 21). Literally, "fear." It includes trembling in the presence of the holy and awareness of impending judgment.

2. In your own words, what motive does verse 21 provide for Paul's command?

   _____

   _____

   _____

   _____

3. What are some of the practical implications of this motive in verse 21 for

   those in authority? _____

   _____

   _____

_____

_____

_____

_____

those under authority? _____

_____

_____

_____

_____

_____

_____

For Further Study: A concordance will lead you to other teaching on authority and submission if you look up words like *respect, honor, submit, fear, obey, love, serve, elder(s), shepherd(s), submit, subordinate,* etc. A Bible dictionary will clarify the meanings of these words. Be sure to pay attention to the context of the verses you find—what is the author's point in the whole chapter?

Marriage

4. In the chart below, record the attitudes that Paul taught each spouse to have toward the other (verses 21-33).

Wives	Husbands
(21) submit out of reverence for Christ	(21) submit out of reverence for Christ
(22)	(25-27)
(23)	

93

Wives	Husbands
(24)	(28-29)
(33)	(33)

5. In verses 23-24, Paul sets up an analogy between husband and wife and Christ and the Church.

   a. In the context of this analogy, what do you think the concept of headship means?

   _____

   _____

   _____

   _____

   _____

   b. What does the concept of a wife's submission mean in the context of this analogy?

   _____

   _____

   _____

   _____

   _____

   _____

   _____

6. Read 5:25-30. Why do you think Paul used Christ and His body/Church as an illustration of how husbands are to love their wives?

_____

_____

_____

_____

_____

_____

For Thought and Discussion: In Paul's day, wives were their husbands' property. Both law and public opinion judged it normal for a man to beat his wife. How did Paul's counsel to husbands differ from the norms of society?

Ought: (verse 28). Or, "owe it [to God and man]."[3]

7. a. How would submission "as to the Lord" and "out of reverence for Christ" have differed from an Ephesian wife's customary submission?

_____

_____

_____

_____

_____

_____

b. How does it differ from your society's advice to wives?

_____

_____

_____

_____

_____

For Thought and Discussion: Look again at Paul's analogy between husband and wife, and Christ and the Church. In areas such as headship, submission, and sacrificial love, how far do you think Paul intended this analogy to be taken? Think about *why* Paul made this analogy, as well as the possible limitations he intended the Ephesians to be aware of in this comparison.

For Thought and Discussion: If your spouse is not living up to Paul's commands, are you free to stop loving or submitting? Why? How can love and submission express themselves in such a case? (See also Luke 6:27-38 and 1 Peter 3:1-8.)

8. Why do you think Paul adds the image of union, in verses 31-32? What does this contribute to the comparison he has been building from verse 23 on?

_____

_____

_____

_____

_____

_____

9. Summarize the attitudes that husband and wife should have toward each other, according to Paul's statement in 5:33.

_____

_____

_____

_____

_____

_____

_____

10. a. What do you think are the most important keys Paul provides to a wife's proper understanding of submission to her husband?

_____

_____

_____

_____

_____

_____

_____

b. to a husband's proper understanding of love for his wife?

_____

_____

_____

_____

_____

_____

11. Has there been any insight or discovery in your study of Ephesians 5:21-33 that you think God may be using to prompt you to change—especially in areas such as thoughts, attitudes, or behavior? If so, write it down here.

_____

_____

_____

_____

_____

_____

12. a. State the main teaching of 5:21-33.

_____

_____

_____

_____

b. How does this passage relate to 4:1-5:20?

_____

_____

For Further Study:
a. Genesis 2:18-20 explains why God made woman. What does the phrase "suitable helper" (verse 20) imply to you about woman's purpose?
b. Genesis 2:21-24 describes how God made woman. What do you learn from that passage about the relationship God intended man and woman to have? (See also Genesis 1:27.)

Optional Application: Memorize verse 21, and meditate on its implications for your relationships with other people—spouse, family members, church members, friends and acquaintances, and so forth.

_____
_____
_____
_____
_____

13. List any questions you have about 5:21-33.

_____
_____
_____
_____
_____
_____

For the group

Whether or not marriage seems important to your group, help everyone to grasp Paul's concept of submission to one another. Consider submission in light of chapters 1-3—the Christian's identity.

Be sure to invite members' questions. (The question of how to deal with an abusive spouse, if it comes up, may be especially difficult.) The commentaries on pages 123-124 may answer some; for others try Elisabeth Elliot's *Shadow of the Almighty*, John and Paula Sandford's *Restoring the Christian Family*, or some other book on this subject.

1. Barth, page 708.
2. Barth, page 710.
3. Barth, page 631.

EPHESIANS 6:1-9

Submission 2

Read 6:1-9, and review the meaning of the word *submission* from lesson 11.

Children

1. What do you think it means to obey "in the Lord" (verse 1)?

_____

_____

_____

_____

_____

2. Explain what you think it means to "honor" parents.

_____

_____

_____

_____

_____

For Thought and Discussion: Do you think the command to honor parents applies only to minors, or also to adults? Why?

Optional Application: Think about your attitudes toward your parents. (In order to identify them, you may need to take a few minutes for reflective thought and prayer.)
a. Describe any dishonoring attitudes you have had or may still have toward them.
b. What do you think you should do now about these attitudes? To help you answer, look up Matthew 6:14-15, 1 John 1:9-10, and 1 John 2:9-11.

3. a. What is the "promise" that Paul quotes along with the commandment (verse 3; see also Deuteronomy 5:16)?

_____

_____

_____

_____

b. Why do you think God put this commandment together with this promise? What connection do you see between them?

_____

_____

_____

_____

_____

_____

Parents

4. What things do you think Paul had in mind when he commanded fathers not to "exasperate" (provoke to anger) their children (verse 4)?

_____

_____

_____

_____

_____

5. Describe how a father might train (discipline) and instruct his children in a manner "of the Lord" (verse 4).

_____

_____

_____

_____

_____

6. How should verse 4 affect a parent's attitudes and behavior toward his or her children? Try to be specific.

_____

_____

_____

_____

_____

_____

For Thought and Discussion: Why do you think Paul addressed *fathers* rather than both parents in verse 4?

Slaves

7. Think about the situation Paul was addressing in 6:5-9. What do you think it means to "obey . . . with respect and fear, and with sincerity of heart, just as you would obey Christ" (verse 5)?

_____

_____

_____

_____

8. How do verses 6 and 7 explain Paul's instruction in verse 5?

_____

_____

_____

_____

101

**Optional Applica-
tion:** a. List your
motives for working
(either in or out of the
home). Try to be as
honest as possible.
b. In what ways do you
live up and fail to live
up to the kind of
mindset Paul wanted
slaves to have?

**For Thought and Dis-
cussion:** What to you
is most difficult about
the motives for work-
ing or serving that Paul
teaches in 6:5-8?

9. a. What do you think are the kinds of attitudes
Paul wanted to teach slaves by the promise he
stated in verse 8?

_____

_____

_____

_____

_____

_____

 b. What wrong attitudes do you think he was trying to steer them away from?

_____

_____

_____

_____

_____

10. To what extent do you think Paul's teaching for
slaves applies to modern people employed for
wages or serving in the home? Why?

_____

_____

_____

_____

_____

Masters

11. To what treatment does "in the same way" refer in
verse 9? (NASB reads, "masters, do the same things
to them.")

_____

_____

_____

_____

_____

12. Describe the attitudes a master should not have, according to verse 9.

_____

_____

_____

_____

_____

_____

13. What fact should a person in authority always keep in mind when dealing with subordinates (verse 9)?

_____

_____

_____

_____

_____

14. To whom in your day might Paul's commands to masters apply?

_____

_____

_____

_____

_____

For Thought and Discussion: How should a Christian respond to directions he (or she) finds unpleasant but not unbiblical from those in authority over him? (See, for instance, 1 Peter 2:13-17.) What about directions he believes are unbiblical (Acts 4:19)?

For Thought and Discussion: Look at your answer to question 13. Within organizations, in what ways should people be treated the same? In what ways is it fair to treat them differently?

For Further Study:
Make up your own outline of 5:21-6:9.

Optional Application: Even if you have no formally established subordinates, you probably oversee other people from time to time—such as baby sitters, newspaper deliverers, repairmen, housekeepers, people in your church or in a small group Bible study, and so forth. How can you show the attitudes taught in 6:9 to those you supervise?

Summary

15. State the central teaching of 6:1-9, and explain how the passage relates to chapter 5.

_____

_____

_____

_____

_____

_____

_____

16. Is there an area of your thought or behavior that you have been convicted of in your study of authority and submission? If so, write it down, along with anything you might do this week to put your desire for obedience into action.

_____

_____

_____

_____

_____

_____

_____

17. List any questions you have about 6:1-9.

_____

_____

_____

_____

_____

_____

For the group

Look for ways to practice submission within your group. How could other members help you in the applications you want to make?

You might want to take one meeting to discuss the parent-child relationship and one to discuss ethics in the work-place. Again, keep the motives and self-image of chapters 1-3 in mind.

Optional Application: Memorize 6:2-3, or any other verses from this passage that you think God most desires you to take to heart this week.

105

LESSON THIRTEEN

EPHESIANS 6:10-20

Spiritual Warfare

Before reading 6:10-20 several times, review Paul's discussion so far in Ephesians about God's purpose for
Creation and the Church.

1. Paul said that "our struggle is not against flesh
   and blood," but against "spiritual forces," or spiritual beings (verse 12). For what goal was Paul
   struggling? (Compare 3:8-10 and 2 Corinthians
   10:3-5.)

   _____

   _____

   _____

   _____

   _____

   _____

2. What do you think it means to "be strong in the
   Lord and in his mighty power" (verse 10)?

   _____

   _____

   _____

   _____

   _____

3. What is Paul's counsel in verse 11 (also in verse 13) for engaging in the struggle defined in verse 12?

_____

_____

_____

_____

_____

Preparation

Can: (verse 11). Literally, "will have power."

Stand your ground: (verse 13). A military term meaning either "to take over," "to hold a watchpost," or "to . . . hold out in a critical position on a battlefield."[1]

It is not possible to "stand your ground" without having "done everything" (verse 13). Consider the use of each of the pieces of armor Paul described.

4. *With the belt of truth buckled around your waist* (verse 14) is literally "having girded your loins with truth" (NASB). (A man tucked his garment into his belt when he needed his legs free for battle.) What do you think it means to "gird your loins with truth"?

_____

_____

_____

_____

_____

5. Why is this piece of preparation important in resisting evil?

_____

_____

_____

_____

_____

Righteousness: (verse 14). Truth, righteousness, faith, etc. are the gifts that God promised in His covenant and the signs of His kingdom. (See Isaiah 59:15-21, especially verse 17). Thus, "righteousness" is the righteousness of God, the salvation and judgment to be fully manifest when the Messiah returns. Also, in the Old Testament, one who "puts on" righteousness accepts the high calling of a righteous judge—that is, the responsibility to see justice done on earth.[2]

6. Explain what you think it means to put on righteousness as a breastplate.

_____

_____

_____

_____

_____

7. Why are you vulnerable to attack if you are not "wearing" true righteousness?

_____

_____

_____

_____

_____

8. What are some practical implications of the image
   in verse 14?

   _____

   _____

   _____

   _____

   _____

Readiness: (verse 15). Probably "steadfastness"[3] or
stability, as with firm boots.

---

9. The "gospel of peace" (Ephesians 6:15, compare
   Isaiah 52:7) is the good news of wholeness and
   reconciliation through Christ. How does this good
   news provide stable support in your warfare?

   _____

   _____

   _____

   _____

   _____

10. a. What do you think "faith" in verse 16 means?

    _____

    _____

    _____

    _____

    b. Explain what you think "the flaming arrows of
       the evil one" (verse 16) are, and how faith can
       extinguish them.

    _____

    _____

110

_____

_____

_____

_____

Optional Application: When you encounter challenges in the form of people, temptations, or tasks to fulfill, which parts of your armor are weak? Which are strong? Describe how you could strengthen each piece of your armor:
truth
righteousness
the gospel of peace
faith
salvation
the word of God

11. What do you think "the helmet of salvation" (verse 17) refers to?

_____

_____

_____

_____

_____

12. How does the helmet of salvation protect you from evil attack?

_____

_____

_____

_____

_____

Word: (verse 17). Probably not just the Old Testament Scriptures, but also the preaching of the gospel and prayer.

13. In what ways is the word of God—"the sword of the Spirit"—an offensive and a defensive weapon?

_____

_____

_____

_____

111

14. The command in verse 18 is both a continuation
    of the armor which protects the Christian from evil
    and a description of his manner of warfare.
    (Remember that the sword of the Spirit is both
    offensive and defensive.) Why do you think Paul
    wraps up his discussion of "the full armor of God"
    with this command (verse 18)?

    _____

    _____

    _____

    _____

    _____

15. List the five instructions on how to pray given in
    verse 18. After each, explain the specific instruc-
    tion in your own words. Put a star by any of the
    instructions you are not sure you practice.

    a. _____

    _____

    _____

    _____

    _____

    b. _____

    _____

    _____

    _____

    _____

    c. _____

    _____

    _____

    _____

d. _____

_____

_____

_____

_____

e. _____

_____

_____

_____

_____

16. Why is the work of prayer so crucial?

_____

_____

_____

_____

_____

_____

17. a. "Fearlessly" in verses 19 and 20 can also mean with "good humor" or "high spirits."[4] How did Paul want the Ephesians to pray for him? To answer, pretend you were in the Ephesian church, and write out a one or two sentence prayer for Paul.

_____

_____

_____

_____

_____

_____

_____

_____

b. Why do you think Paul asked the Ephesians for this kind of prayer?

_____

_____

_____

_____

_____

18. What does Paul's prayer request in 6:19-20 suggest for

a. our intercession for those actively spreading the gospel?

_____

_____

_____

_____

_____

b. our own presentation of the gospel to unbelievers?

_____

_____

_____

_____

_____

19. a. State the main point of 6:10-20.

_____

_____

_____

_____

_____

b. How does 6:10-20 relate to Paul's purpose for writing the letter?

_____

_____

_____

_____

_____

For Further Study: Make up an outline for 6:10-20.

Optional Application: Are there any other responses to 6:10-20 that you have, perhaps involving some further action or change on your part?

Following Paul's example

Note the connection between the form of the letter to Ephesus and the main work of a Christian. Notice especially the proportion of space Paul gave to prayer for his own needs as opposed to praise, thanksgiving, prayer for God's will to be done, and prayer for others' needs. (Compare Jesus' model in Matthew 6:9-13.)

20. What are some ways that you could apply the lessons on prayer in this passage?

_____

_____

_____

_____

_____

_____

_____

115

For the group

You may need two meetings for everyone to see what battle we are engaged in, why each piece of armor is important, and how you should pray. It might be productive to spend a whole meeting discussing what Ephesians teaches about prayer, why it is important, and how you can practice it. However, if your time is limited, you could omit going over each piece of armor in detail (questions 4-13).

The assumptions of modern culture hinder the idea that crime, family tensions, war, social injustice, sickness, etc. are all connected to a spiritual war that must be fought according to Ephesians 6:10-20. Work to see the connection.

After you discuss the purpose of intercessory prayer and its methods, consider committing yourselves to practicing it together. Remember that Paul was writing to whole congregations, not to individuals, about the work of the Church.

Paul also expected that Christians would be helping one another to stand firm and to repair their armor. How can others in your group help you? How can you help them?

1. Barth, page 762.
2. Barth, pages 795-797.
3. Barth, page 770.
4. Barth, page 777.

EPHESIANS 6:21-24 AND REVIEW

Looking Back

1. What do you learn from 6:21-24 about relationships among Christians in the early Church? List as many observations as you can.

_____

_____

_____

_____

_____

_____

_____

_____

Study Skill—Listing Observations
When you study the Bible without a study guide, this procedure of making observations and writing them down should always be your first step. After listing everything you observe, even things that seem trivial, you will begin asking yourself who, what, when, where, how, and why questions like those in this study guide. You will find the cross-references and word definitions yourself, using whatever study aids you need to help.

Review

2. Reread Paul's letter, and discuss here what you think were the most important lessons you learned from it. Summarize your findings according to

who you are in Christ

_____

_____

_____

_____

_____

_____

God's goal for the church

_____

_____

_____

_____

_____

the believer's mission

_____

_____

_____

_____

_____

how you should live in light of your identity

_____

_____

_____

_____

_____

_____

how you become able to live as God wants

_____

_____

_____

_____

_____

_____

prayer

_____

_____

_____

_____

_____

other topics

_____

_____

_____

_____

_____

3. Look back at the questions you listed at the ends of lessons one through thirteen. Do any questions that seem important to you remain unanswered? If

For Further Study:
Now try to see the book as a whole. From your overview in lesson one, your summary statements in each lesson, any outlining you did, and a final reading of the letter, try to outline it.

1) At the top of a sheet of paper, write what you think the book's purpose is.

2) Let your two main divisions be chapters 1-3 and 4-6.

3) Fill in the supporting sections in each division and the paragraphs in each section. Consult the chart on page 19 only if you get stuck.

so, some of the sources on pages 123-127 may help you to answer those questions. Or, you might study some particular passage with cross-references on your own.

4. Have you noticed any areas (thoughts, attitudes, opinions, behavior) in which you have changed as a result of studying Paul's letter to the Ephesian church? If so, explain how you have changed.

_____

_____

_____

_____

_____

_____

_____

_____

_____

5. Look back over the entire study at questions in which you expressed a desire to make some specific personal application. Are you satisfied with your follow-through? Pray about any of those areas that you think you should continue to pursue specifically. (Now that you have completed this study, perhaps something new has come to mind that you would like to concentrate on. If so, bring it before God in prayer as well.) Write any notes here.

_____

_____

_____

_____

_____

_____

_____

For the group

After covering the questions in this lesson, let anyone pose any questions he still has about the book. See if you can plan how to answer them.

Then, evaluate how well your group functioned during your study of Ephesians. (You may want to take a whole meeting for this.) Some questions you might ask are:

What did you learn about small group study?
How well did you act like the body of Christ?
What needs of members did the group meet?
What needs did the group fail to meet, and how might it do better in future?
Was everyone able to share ideas?
Was your corporate prayer time fruitful?
What are members' current needs? What will you do next?

STUDY AIDS

For further information on the material covered in this study, you might consider the following sources. If your local bookstore does not have them, you can have the bookstore order them from the publisher, or you can find them in most seminary libraries. Many university and public libraries will also carry these books.

Commentaries on Ephesians

Barth, Markus. *Ephesians 1-3* and *Ephesians 4-6* (Anchor Bible Series, Volumes 34 and 34A, Doubleday, 1974).
>An exhaustive two-volume phrase-by-phrase analysis. Addresses most textual issues. Especially good on word meanings and the culture of the day. Readable for the layman; no Greek necessary. Markus Barth is more evangelically conservative than his father, Karl. This is one of the better works in the Anchor Series.

Bruce, F.F. *The Epistles to the Colossians, to Philemon, and to the Ephesians* (New International Commentary on the New Testament, Eerdmans, 1984).
>Excellent on theology, word studies, and cross-references. Very good introduction to the setting in the Lycus Valley region of Asia Minor. Although Greek references and footnotes make it scholarly, a person can learn a great deal about Paul's message without knowledge of Greek.

Foulkes, Francis. *The Epistle of Paul to the Ephesians* (Tyndale New Testament Commentary, Eerdmans, 1981).
>Much shorter than Barth or Hodge, but longer than Bruce. Touches most major points regarding the language and ideas of Paul's letter. Very accessible to a beginning student. First published in 1956. Available in an inexpensive paperback edition.

Hendriksen, William. *Exposition of Galatians-Ephesians* (Baker, 1981).
   Very readable and inspiring, like good expository sermons on the text of Paul's letter. Hendriksen is concerned to show the letter's relevance to modern Christians.

Hodge, Charles. *A Commentary on the Epistle to the Ephesians* (Baker, 1980).
   An inexpensive paperback reprint of the classic 1856 original. Learned phrase-by-phrase analysis on the level of Barth and Bruce. Refers extensively to Greek, but non-Greek scholars should have little trouble.

Stott, John. *God's New Society: The Message of Ephesians* (The Bible Speaks Today Series, InterVarsity, 1980).
   Stott expounds the text of the letter and applies it to the modern world. His theme is Paul's vision of the Church.

Historical Sources

Bruce, F.F. *New Testament History* (Doubleday, 1979).
   A readable history of Herodian kings, Roman governors, philosophical schools, Jewish sects, Jesus, the early Jerusalem church, Paul, and early gentile Christianity. Well-documented with footnotes for the serious student, but the notes do not intrude.

Bruce, F.F. *Paul, Apostle of the Heart Set Free* (Eerdmans, 1977).
   Possibly the best book around on Paul's personality and ideas set in their historical context. Excellent both on Paul's teaching and his times. Very readable.

Harrison, E.F. *Introduction to the New Testament* (Eerdmans, 1971).
   History from Alexander the Great—who made Greek culture dominant in the biblical world—through philosophies, pagan and Jewish religion, Jesus' ministry and teaching (the weakest section), and the spread of Christianity. Very good maps and photographs of the land, art, and architecture of New Testament times.

Concordances, Dictionaries, and Handbooks

A *concordance* lists words of the Bible alphabetically along with each verse in which the word appears. It lets you do your own word studies. An *exhaustive* concordance lists every word used in a given translation, while an *abridged* or *complete* concordance omits either some words, some occurrences of the word, or both.
   The two best exhaustive concordances are *Strong's Exhaustive Concordance* and *Young's Analytical Concordance to the Bible.* Both are based on the King James Version of the Bible. *Strong's* has an index by which you can find out which Greek or Hebrew word is used in a given English verse. *Young's*

breaks up each English word it translates. However, neither concordance requires knowledge of the original language.

Among other good, less expensive concordances, *Cruden's Complete Concordance* is keyed to the King James and Revised Versions, and *The NIV Complete Concordance* is keyed to the New International Version. These include all references to every word included, but they omit "minor" words. They also lack indexes to the original languages.

A *Bible dictionary* or *Bible encyclopedia* alphabetically lists articles about people, places, doctrines, important words, customs, and geography of the Bible.

The New Bible Dictionary, edited by J.D. Douglas, F.F. Bruce, J.I. Packer, N. Hillyer, D. Gutherie, A.R. Millard, and D.J. Wiseman (Tyndale, 1982) is more comprehensive than most dictionaries. Its 1300 pages include quantities of information along with excellent maps, charts, diagrams, and an index for cross-referencing.

Unger's Bible Dictionary by Merrill F. Unger (Moody, 1979) is equally excellent and is available in an inexpensive paperback edition.

The Zondervan Pictorial Encyclopedia edited by Merrill C. Tenney (Zondervan, 1975, 1976) is excellent and exhaustive. It is being revised and updated in the 1980's. However, its five 1000-page volumes are a financial investment, so all but very serious students may prefer to use it at a library.

Unlike a Bible dictionary in the above sense, *Vine's Expository Dictionary of New Testament Words* by W.E. Vine (various publishers) alphabetically lists major words used in the King James Version and defines each New Testament Greek word that KJV translates with that English word. *Vine's* lists verse references where that Greek word appears, so that you can do your own cross-references and word studies without knowing any Greek.

A good *Bible atlas* can be a great aid to understanding what is going on in a book of the Bible and how geography affected events. Here are a few good choices.

The MacMillan Atlas by Yohanan Aharoni and Michael Avi-Yonah (MacMillan, 1968, 1977) contains 264 maps, 89 photos, and 12 graphics. The many maps of individual events portray battles, movements of people, and changing boundaries in detail.

The New Bible Atlas by J.J. Bimson and J.P. Kane (Tyndale, 1984) has 73 maps, 34 photos, and 34 graphics. Its evangelical perspective, concise and helpful text, and excellent research make it a very good choice, but its greatest strength is its outstanding graphics, such as cross-sections of the Dead Sea.

The Bible Mapbook by Simon Jenkins (Lion, 1984) is much shorter and less expensive than most other atlases, and so it is a good first taste of the usefulness of maps. It contains 91 simple maps, very little text, and 20 graphics. Some of the graphics are computer-generated and intriguing.

The Moody Atlas of Bible Lands by Barry J. Beitzel (Moody, 1984) is scholarly, very evangelical, and fully of theological text, indexes, and references. This admirable reference work will be too deep and costly for some, but Beitzel shows vividly how God prepared the land of Israel perfectly for the acts of salvation He was going to accomplish in it.

A *handbook* of bible customs can also be useful. Some good ones are *Today's Handbook of Bible Times and Customs* by William L. Coleman (Bethany, 1984) and the less detailed *Daily Life in Bible Times* (Nelson, 1982).

For Small Group Leaders

The Small Group Leader's Handbook by Steve Barker et al. (InterVarsity, 1982).
    Written by an InterVarsity small group with college students primarily in mind. It includes information on group dynamics and how to lead in light of them, and many ideas for worship, building community, and outreach. It has a good chapter on doing inductive Bible study.

Getting Together: A Guide for Good Groups by Em Griffin (InterVarsity, 1982).
    Applies to all kinds of groups, not just Bible studies. From his own experience, Griffin draws deep insights into why people join groups; how people relate to each other; and principles of leadership, decision-making, and discussions. It is fun to read, but its 229 pages will take more time than the above book.

You Can Start a Bible Study Group by Gladys Hunt (Harold Shaw, 1984).
    Builds on Hunt's thirty years of experience leading groups. This book is wonderfully focused on God's enabling. It is both clear and applicable for Bible study groups of all kinds.

How to Lead Small Groups by Neal F. McBride (NavPress, 1990).
    Covers leadership skills for all kinds of small groups—Bible study, fellowship, task, and support groups. Filled with step-by-step guidance and practical exercises to help you grasp the critical aspects of small group leadership and dynamics.

The Small Group Letter, a special section in Discipleship Journal (NavPress).
    Unique. Its four pages per issue, six issues per year are packed with practical ideas for small groups. It stays up to date because writers discuss what they are currently doing as small group members and leaders. To subscribe, write to Subscription Services, Post Office Box 54470, Boulder, Colorado 80323-4470.

Bible Study Methods

Braga, James, *How to Study the Bible* (Multnomah, 1982).
    Clear chapters on a variety of approaches to Bible study: synthetic, geographical, cultural, historical, doctrinal, practical, and so on. Designed to help the ordinary person without seminary training to use these approaches.

Fee, Gordon, and Douglas Stuart. *How to Read the Bible For All Its Worth* (Zondervan, 1982).
    After explaining in general what interpretation (exegesis) and application (hermeneutics) are, Fee and Stuart offer chapters on interpreting and applying the different kinds of writing in the Bible: Epistles, Gospels, Old Testament Law, Old Testament narrative, the Prophets, Psalms, Wisdom, and Revelation. Fee and Stuart also suggest good commentaries on each biblical book. They write as conservative scholars who personally recognize Scripture as God's Word for their daily lives.

Jensen, Irving L. *Independent Bible Study* (Moody, 1963), and *Enjoy Your Bible* (Moody, 1962).
    The former is a comprehensive introduction to the inductive Bible study method, especially the use of synthetic charts. The latter is a simpler introduction to the subject.

Wald, Oletta. *The Joy of Discovery in Bible Study* (Augsburg, 1975).
    Wald focuses on issues such as how to observe all that is in a text, how to ask questions of a text, how to use grammar and passage structure to see the writer's point, and so on. Very helpful on these subjects.

Other titles in the
Lifechange series
you may be interested in: